PORT to PORT

PORT to PORT

Personal memories of people, places and the sea

David Houghton

Copyright © David Houghton 2023

All rights reserved. The right of David Houghton to be identified as the author of this work has been asserted in accordance with the Copyright, Designs, and Patents act 1988. No part of this publication may be altered, reproduced, distributed, or transmitted in any form, by any means, including but not limited to scanning, duplicating, or reselling, without permission of the publisher, except in the case of reasonable quotations in features such as reviews, interviews, and certain other non-commercial uses currently permitted by copyright law.

Dedication

This book is dedicated to Andy Thompson and Phil Cheeseborough. My partners in crime, without whom most of these events would never have occurred.

You are the only people accurately named on these pages because someone has to share the blame.

Apology

I have chosen an easy conversational writing style for friends and family to enjoy. I apologise to all grammar police for starting sentences with I, poor punctuation, and generally breaking the strict rules of written English in many ways.

CONTENTS

FOREWORD	3
TAXI FOR PETER	5
WHAT'S OCCURRING	22
A FLIGHT OF FANCY.	36
DON'T TRY THIS AT HOME	54
THE ORIGIN OF SPECIES	62
CRAZY FROG	76
LAND OF MILK AND HONEY	81
SWIMMING WITH THE FISHES	89
MAN OVERBOARD	93
OOH, LA LA!	100
GUNS AND PIZZA	107
THE PERFECT CRIME	111
CHICAGO OR BUST	115
P IS FOR Pis…a	122
DON'T GO INTO THE LIGHT	128
ST. JOHNS SURPRISE	134
HOLY F**K	139
TURBO CURRY	145
FOOLS AND HORSES	153
THE GODFATHER	159
CAN I HAVE A VODKA WITH THAT?	166
A LETTER FROM VALLETTA	179
SEAGOING SCHEDULE	192-201

FOREWORD

I joined the Merchant Navy as a Cadet with Shaw Saville in 1974. By 1984 I had my Chief Engineers Certificate, but after ten years, my career at sea was over. Impending marriage was one reason, but the other was the decline of the British Merchant Fleet. I had already handed over two ships to foreign owners and sailed one trip under a foreign flag. The job and ships were the same, but the spirit and banter were missing.

I have tried to capture the spirit and banter that made life at sea so special in this series of small memoirs from my short but varied career. In ten years, I circumnavigated the globe by air and sea, seeing wonderful sights but, more importantly, meeting wonderful people.

These stories are not just about my fellow seafarers but also about the local people we met along the way. They are as accurate as I can remember, but most names have been omitted or changed to protect the innocent and potential lawsuits. If you recognise yourself, please let me know. I would love to hear if your recollection matches mine or if you have enjoyed reading my favourite memories about my time at sea.

I suspect the fact that you have this book means that you already know I can be contacted via the Elders & Fyffes or Shaw Savill Facebook groups.

TAXI FOR PETER

Only twenty-four hours earlier I had described our destination as the arsehole of the world. Now I was cheering as we accepted the telegraph signal to stop engines alongside the dock in Sheerness.

The saving grace was that Sheerness is in Kent, Kent is in England and we had been at sea for six weeks since loading seven thousand tonnes of apples in Tasmania. Not that the trip there or back had been boring, quite the opposite. Fyffes was a relatively new company to me and I did not expect my second trip to start with a long-haul flight to Tasmania to join a ship.

Flying from Heathrow to Tasmania, an island south of the Australian mainland, is about as long haul as you can get without actually being on your way back to Heathrow again. Flying there in 36 hours was tiring, but returning by ship took considerably longer. Starting in the Tasman Sea, then via the Indian Ocean, Arabian Sea, Gulf of Aden, Red Sea, Suez Canal, Mediterranean Sea, the Strait of Gibraltar, North Atlantic, English Channel, North Sea and finally the Thames Estuary, was a long trip without setting foot ashore.

Things were very different now. The exotic locations and sunshine were gone, but the promise of getting onto dry land for the first time in six weeks was very welcome.

As we stopped the engines, the engineers ran to the deck to see the view. "Don't get excited. There is nothing to see", I shouted as they left me alone to carry out the arrival checks. My job as a junior engineer was to prepare the engine room after docking for the evening and then hand it over to the unlucky junior on the fourteen-hour night watch.

My comment was not unusual as most dock areas are similar, with warehouses, cranes and little more worthy of note.

However, it is only fair to exclude the Central American banana ports from that description. They were not docks but simple jetties, often alongside a picturesque town sitting inside beautiful jungle-covered bays. The fact that they were generally swathed in beautiful sunshine also helped the feel-good factor.

There was no such feel-good factor for the engineers as they gazed over the rail towards the dockside of Sheerness. Kent in winter was not swathed in sunshine. Giant grey cranes hung over the ship like the Martians from War of the Worlds fame as the rain poured down, forming large oily puddles across the quayside. The rainwater was not dripping but flowing off every warehouse roof and broken gutter, adding to the greyness of the buildings. However, nothing would dampen the crew's enthusiasm because they were home in England and could go to an authentic pub and get real fish and chips.

Apart from the Captain and Chief Engineer who had 'been there and done it many times before', the officer's mess was empty that evening. Everybody who could be was washed, dressed and off into town. Unlike most of my counterparts, I had been to Sheerness before with my previous company. So, I knew not to expect too much from the evening, but I was still excited at the prospect of real beer and fish and chips.

It had stopped raining when we were ready, and I knew the walk into town was only about twenty minutes. Still, the general consensus of opinion was to get taxis. Two came quickly. I knew this was because the train station where they waited was directly outside the dock gates. Sheerness town consisted of a small end-of-line train station and a high street with a choice of several pubs. We got dropped at the far end of the high street to work our way back.

This was an excellent strategic decision for many reasons. The first was that we were always getting closer to the ship as the evening went on, and our walking abilities degenerated. Second, the poshest pubs were at the far end, working towards the Railway Inn, best described as the local pub full of interesting characters. The railway inn was also next to the taxi rank at the station. So that was a nice benefit of our plan. Finally and very importantly, the best chip shop in town was in the middle of the high street, so it was a few pints, some fish and chips, a few more pints, and a taxi back to the ship. The perfect plan, what could go wrong?

Nothing went wrong, but it may have gone too right. Pubs were visited, beers were had and fish and chips were eagerly consumed in the paper as they should be. However, the pubs appeared to drop in standard by a regular percentage the closer we got to the station. At the second to last pub, we ended up talking to some local girls, and when we asked about the next pub, they said they were going there too.

So on to the next pub, the look and feel of the bar at the Railway Inn were similar to a western movie tavern. I could imagine that walking in as a drunken group of strangers would have felt like a scene from High Noon. So, the benefit of walking in with a couple of local girls was instantly appreciated. Our appreciation increased as we were introduced to the bar staff and all the locals in the bar. They immediately made us feel welcome and were genuinely interested in us and our recent trip from Australia.

Within a few drinks, we had become honorary locals, more girls had joined the group and the curtains were closed at some time in the evening, indicating that we were in a lock-in. Closing time was still 10.30 pm for pubs, so it was a surprise when it was suggested it was nearly 1 am and time to go home. Despite hours of drinking and overconsumption, it still seemed like a good idea to invite all our new friends back to the ship's bar for a nightcap. This was especially so because all of our remaining new friends were female. In fact, we were outnumbered male to female by one extra girl who was one of those friends who always hangs on too long when their mate has pulled.

The taxi rank was empty at this late hour, and the rest of Sheerness was in darkness. Once again, the local girls came to our rescue. With a call from the pay phone on the bar, two cabs had appeared outside in no time. The fact that these were four-seater mini cabs was utterly ignored, and somehow thirteen of us squeezed into two cabs for the short journey to the ship. This was definitely before the days of strict car overcrowding rules and the drivers, who were obviously friends of the girls, were more than happy to avoid a return trip. I remember it being a perfect start to the rest of the evening and it helped with the selection process of who may pair off with whom, which seemed so delicate and complicated in the pub.

It was clear that in our easily manipulated drunken state, the girls had organised us into the taxis they had already agreed on in the pub. So that they were conveniently sitting on the laps of the men they had pre-chosen. This was, of course, fine by us. We were drunk and horny and surrounded by young women. These were wiggling on our laps and placing our hands in positions on their person that would typically require several dates and agreed consent in a normal relationship. Although they did not speak the queen's English and their manner was a little direct, they had been pleasant, fun and attractive company for the evening.

I remember the girl sitting on my knee in her early twenties with short blonde hair and a curvy figure, which I now realised meant heavy thighs. Heavy on my knee but very soft to touch, I soon discovered, as she lifted my hand and guided it around her thigh and under the front of her skirt. This was a pleasant surprise. I wondered how to get to the bar and take this to the next level. Suddenly, the next level was delivered literally into my lap. Being as drunk as I was, I didn't really feel self-conscious, but I did check to see if the others had seen my progress so far. I turned to the right to see Phil engaged in a serious case of bra wrangling. To my left, Pete's girl had somehow turned round in the most cramped of spaces and appeared to be eating him alive with little objection from him. The only embarrassing thing happening in the car was the girl sitting in the front seat staring out of the window as she chatted to the driver. I didn't even know whose best friend she was. It turned out later that she was with the man-eater on Pete's lap, who was clearly not distraught at her mate's loneliness and isolation during this mobile backseat sex show.

Arriving at the ship and the bar, we were not surprised to find a few lads still in there, putting the world to rights with a late-night drink. The chief electrician was sitting happily at the end of the bar with his fiancé. She had come to meet him and had been standing on the dockside at our arrival. He would normally be the main party animal leading the drinking, but tonight he was clearly chilled and happy with his girl by his side. He was still utterly drunk as a skunk of course, as was she. You don't change all your habits just because your girlfriend has turned up.

The third mate kept him company as the officer on board, so he had not been allowed ashore that evening. This made him the duty officer, responsible and sober at all times. It was a description that did not fit with his present condition in any way. He struggled to sit on the bar stool and lighting a cigarette was entirely beyond his capabilities.

Nevertheless, when we walked in, he gathered his senses and jumped behind the bar to be the perfect host for the girls. Despite his inebriated state, the gallant action of serving us all drinks had impressed our lonely girl. Soon, she was deep in some drunken exchange that would be hard to describe as conversation. With partners now all matched up and much fondling taking place around the room, it was only a short time before the group started to get smaller, one couple at a time. Eventually, with six of us left as three couples, the conversation was less interesting than the fondling, and we all departed to our beds at about 2 am.

I wish I could say that the sex was wonderful and the earth moved for us, but of course, it didn't. We were both very drunk, and whatever happened was more functional than romantic. Nevertheless, it was nice to wake up the next morning with the touch of a female body next to me. Despite our building hangovers and lack of sleep, we did cuddle as we woke up through the repeated snooze alarms. Her thighs were indeed soft, as was the rest of her, and it made me realise the sacrifice we made and continued to make to have a career at sea. I loved women, everything about them. I loved their touch, their softness, their smell, their shape, their look and their company. Yet this job meant being separated from them for most of our lives.

These escapades written here were just a few lucky times when we managed to connect and enjoy the company of females. The rest of our time was spent in testosterone-fuelled heavy labour and drinking sessions. They were really there to hide our lack of affection and connection with the opposite sex that we so desperately craved.

That morning was the only time at sea I had seen a woman walk out of every cabin on the officer's deck. The melee for tea and toast in the mess room was like a rugby scrum. There was no shortage of either tea or toast. It was just that we never had cups for visitors because we never had visitors! But we all had our loneliness cured, even if just for a short while. Some with their wives and fiancés. The rest of us with the girls of Sheerness who had shown us what a good time could be had and that appearances could be deceptive in what looked like a one-horse town. Even our poor onboard duty man and the loneliest girl in Sheerness managed to find love just for a short time.

I did not return to Sheerness for several trips after that. In between, I wondered if the conversations and stories that grew around that night had coloured my opinion. Were they really the attractive and salt-of-the-earth fun girls we remembered, or was it the alcohol and beer goggles that had made us hitch up with a bunch of trolls? I finally had my chance to find out one evening the following year when Phil and I returned to the scene of the crime.

Sober this time and worried about what to expect, we walked into the Railway Inn. It looked exactly the same as we remembered, but it had probably looked like that for the last 30 years. There were only a few people in there, all men and all uninterested in our arrival. However, there was a man and a woman behind the bar. I recognised the curvy figure and short blonde hair as the girl I had spent the night with on our last visit. My fears were unfounded, she was as attractive as I remember, and I smiled, now feeling self-conscious as I approached the bar. I said "Hi" as I ordered two pints. She looked at me with a slight but quizzical acknowledgement.

I said, "nice to see you again. We were here last year".

You could see her brain processing information as fast as possible before she said. "Bitter?"

"Oh yes, please", I replied, being knocked slightly out of my stride. She placed a glass under the pump and continued.

"Yeh, that was the party on the ship, a good night that. So, you back again, are you?"

"Yes, just for a couple of days", I replied. I was trying to figure out where to take the conversation next. I had not planned past seeing if these girls existed and what they looked like. I was now outside my comfort zone and had no direction from there. She may have sensed my discomfort or simply needed to get rid of hers. Either way, the following line put us both out of our misery. "I work here full time now with Joe, my boyfriend", she said as she gestured towards the gap between the bar and the saloon. A gangly young man in his mid-twenties was talking to a regular about the afternoons' horseracing.

I gasped a sigh of relief internally, hoping it did not show on the outside and said, "that's nice; it should be a good pint then". She smiled as she handed us the glasses and said, "enjoy your pints, lads".

I looked at Phil, and we smiled, ready to enjoy our pints and chat about the old days with renewed confidence. Just then, Peter, the deck cadet, came in and stood beside Phil at the end of the bar.

"Hi, guys," he said.

"Do you want a beer?" I responded, knowing the answer already.

"Yes, please, lager". As the Blonde returned to serve us, Peter nudged Phil. "I know her he said".

"Yes, so do I," said Phil "she was with the group last year. Remember you were with us and very drunk".

"I know, and I missed all the fun because I left, then Tom came back with one of them and shagged her in our cabin while I had to listen".

"Your fault for getting too pissed", Phil responded. The barmaid returned with the lager.

"Here you are, one pint of Carling," she said as she pushed it across the bar.

"Do you know Sara?" He asked her. "My mate met her last year".

"Yes, I know her. She works here part-time", she replied enthusiastically with the type of smile that indicated this was a subject that she was happy to talk about.

"Well, tell her she gave my mate a dose" was Peter's instant, direct and shocking response.

We hadn't seen that coming, and it was a cracker, better described as a hand grenade because all hell let loose. Within a very short time and at full volume, we discovered Sara was her best friend and that she was not a lady to be riled, especially in public. The denials came first, followed by the accusations against us and then the threatened violence, which we heard as we left through the door, leaving three full pints sitting on the bar.

So maybe some of our glasses had been rose-coloured that night the year before, but we agreed it was still a good night as we entered the next pub for a replacement beer.

"Right," we said to Peter, "you little shit, you had better hope none of her friends work here because it's your round, keep your bloody mouth shut, and we are walking back. Definitely no taxis!"

WHAT'S OCCURRING?

"Do you want to top or tail?" was not how I had hoped my evening would end after such a promising start.

When we were sent to the emergency dry dock by the Lloyds insurance inspector, we were surprised to end up in Wales. It surprised us that the little Welsh Holiday Island of Barry had a dry dock. I think it was a surprise to the people of Barry Island as well.

It had all started with a regular engine room inspection by the Lloyds inspector the day before we were scheduled to leave Sheerness. This was similar to a ship MOT to check seaworthiness, and failure could stop the ship from sailing. M.V. Darien was the equivalent of an old banger, held together with epoxy resin, fibreglass tape, and the ever-more creative skills of the engineering team. There was a visible nervousness as the second engineer brought the inspector into the engine room. A routine visit that started with polite pleasantries soon became a long list of red notes on a clipboard and an increasingly concerned look on the face of the inspector. The game was up by the time he reached the main engine seawater coolant pumps.

The high-pressure sea strainer lid had a hole plugged with a wooden bung a metre long and wedged against an adjacent bulkhead frame to stop it from coming out. When the inspector asked why it was there, the third engineer engaged his inner Del Boy. He responded, "It's an additional automatic fire precaution. If there is a fire in the engine room, the wooden bung will burn, and the seawater will extinguish the fire". I swear the inspector was trying to stifle a grin. Still, his red pen scrawled across the clipboard once more, and the Darien was confined to coastal waters until drydocked for repairs.

An indication of the actual state of the ship was that it was entirely seawater cooled, and there were over 30 seawater leaks within the engine room cooling systems. It was clear that a complete renewal was desperately required. That wasn't even the main problem which was actually a crack in the main engine block. So began the search for an immediately available dry dock and a surprise visit to the holiday resort of Barry Island in South Wales.

On our arrival, after the short sailing from Sheerness in Kent, it was clear that the dry dock had been mothballed for some time. The traditional stone dry dock with large wooden gates was surrounded by small abandoned buildings and vintage steam cranes along the side. The cranes had seen better days and had been decommissioned many years ago. However, they still sat motionless, rusting away gently on their rail tracks. Their presence as giant leviathans standing motionless and defeated at the far end of the dock emphasised the sadness and emptiness of this place. Once full of activity, noise, and industry but now neglected, with huge weeds being the only living thing in residence.

No electric cranes had replaced the giants, leaving this as very much an abandoned facility until a mobile crane appeared for the duration of our visit. By comparison, this mobile crane was shiny clean and efficient but always looked like a young gate crasher at a retirement party, showing off. At the same time, the oldies sat back and watched with pride in what they had done and jealousy that their jibs could swing no more.

The local tradesmen were similar to the dry dock themselves. Discarded and neglected after decades of service, they had been left to rot but never fully decommissioned or retrained for new industry. So, they were indeed glad to see us. It had been several years since a ship had graced the dry dock. It was nice to see a little life, vitality and particularly pride being brought back into the local people, even if only for a temporary period of 3 weeks. The workforce was old, but their skills were exemplary. These men knew their trades, and our 20-year-old tired and weary ship, the Darien, was grateful for their skills and knowledge to coax her back into life, just as she was doing for them.

Traditional in their workwear of beige bib and brace overalls and boiler suits. Each day they arrived spot on time, bringing sandwiches in bags and tea in flasks. They stopped for breaks on time and started again on time. In between, they worked tirelessly and expertly using all the skills learnt over decades of hard engineering graft on ships of all sizes and types. After work, they went to the working men's club, where they played darts and drank pints of mild. We know this because it was our first port of call on the walk into town each evening. We were welcomed in like old friends. Each evening we would suffer a pint of awful beer to pay our respects to a workforce of exemplary skills and loyalty that the UK would never see again.

Even by 1980 standards, Barry was a town decades behind the rest of the country. All that was missing was the Hovis boy on his delivery bike to make the picture complete. Whilst the town and industry were traditional, the holiday area was certainly not so. Just a couple of miles away stood the Butlin's Holiday Camp which had made Barry Island the go-to holiday destination for South Wales. But, like the town, the camp was also starting to look dated and tired. The rows of chalets that looked like army barracks, all surrounded by a huge barbed wire fence, did not create the best first impression for the modern 1980s holiday maker. Add to that a daily regimented routine that had seen little change since Billy Butlin started it all in the 1950s. So, it's not hard to understand why the camp eventually closed its doors for the last time in 1996.

Our first visit to Butlins was planned as a joyous trip into a world of beer, fun and girls. The plan was to get in or over the fence to enjoy the delights that this magical holiday world had to offer the less than discerning and let's face it, sometimes desperate young men who spent many lonely months at sea. Well, it had been a whole 24 hours sailing from Sheerness.

Our plan fell at the first hurdle. The hurdle, or security fence, as Butlins would call it, was too big and strong. So, we opted for the easy way in and paid a daily entrance fee to the gateman. We could use all the facilities and fairground rides to get value for money. So straight to the bar where the first surprise came, our suspicions that this was a mistake started to rise. It was less of a bar than a vast hall which would not have been a problem if it were full of young ladies, but it wasn't. It wasn't full of anyone. Just a few families with screaming kids, grannies and a five-foot panda trying but failing to keep it all cheerful.

The real problem came next. The beer was so expensive and poor that we only had one and wandered to find the facilities. Here, I picked up an admirer in the form of a Panda.

Unable to speak, it directed me to the swimming pool and fairground rides with one arm while patting my bum with the other and squeezing me. Assuming this was something it did to everyone, I continued on my way. At this stage, we realised we may have wasted our entrance fee. The pool was in front of us with one hardy soul swimming.

The rest of it, however, was a ghost town. Yes, this was August, but this was also South Wales, and an outside pool in a windswept courtyard by the sea was not what we had signed up for. The Panda expressed little emotion at our plight but did turn us around with its arms wide as if to say here are the fairground rides. The Panda was now utilising all its best mime skills by doubling over as if laughing whilst waving both arms in the air and then holding its stomach and rocking back and forth. Inside the costume, I knew this little sod was laughing its head off as the four of us stared across the concrete square. In front of us was a roundabout with little cars and a Tea Cup ride slowly turning in the distance. There was just one child on each and an unhappy mother slowly and reluctantly spinning in a teacup with her offspring that looked just as reluctant to be there.

The Panda hugged me as if in sympathy and squeezed my bum again. Then, realising our mistake, we headed back to the bar to make our action plan. As we discussed the error of our ways and drowned our sorrows with the barman, it became clear that we had made two huge assumptions that were completely wrong. We needed to reverse them with immediate effect. The first was that all the action was in Butlins when in reality, all the action was outside. Even the people staying in Butlins only slept here.

The best facilities, eating, beer, and fairground rides were all outside. More importantly for us, so were all the women. The second and more critical was my hope that I might have hit it off with the Panda and could get a date with the girl inside. I told the barman all about the hugs, and he confirmed he knew the person in the Panda, which meant they fancied you if you were interested. He then asked if I wanted to pass my interest on to him. Yes, the Panda was a male, so I had willingly been molested by a man. If only operation Yewtree had been around in 1980.

Barry still had so much more to offer us as we ventured out into the real world and the bars and chip shops of the Barry Island Resort. A fairground, some arcades, a few pubs, and chip shops were the sum total of the Resort. Still, they were busy and lively and a world apart from the Butlins Prison Camp experience.

Whilst most holidaymakers were English and Welsh, we did come across the occasional one from further afield. Andy and I met two of these foreigners one late evening in the only Chinese takeaway in town. Andy was a good-looking six-footer with a Magnum Moustache, which, you will have to trust me, was considered attractive and fashionable in 1980. I was the one that hung out with the good-looking one to pick up the scraps, but on this occasion, there were no scraps, just two gorgeous Swedish girls. We didn't so much pick up the girls as their backpacks.

Standing in the takeaway queue behind two of the biggest backpacks we had seen, we offered to take them off as they searched for a map in the depths of their bags. It turned out that they had nowhere to stay and were looking for somewhere to put up a tent at 11.30 at night. How could we let these two young, cute, blonde Swedish girls go into the night alone and lost?

So far, so good. Takeaway bought, Andy and I were walking back to the ship with Swedish Girls in tow and a heavy backpack each as we did the gentlemanly thing for the ladies. They asked about the hill opposite the dry dock as we approached the ship. This may have been the only freely available grassed area in Barry, but it was on a very exposed, steep slope. We recommended to the girls that this was not a good idea and that they should come back with us. They complied for now, at least. Then agreed to venture onto the ship for a beer in the bar. But more out of curiosity than desire.

The bar stragglers perked up considerably as two young women walked in. Within minutes, the bar was repopulated with bleary-eyed men just popping in for a nightcap. The competition was tough, so we took our drinks and some music to the monkey island. To landlubbers, that is the deck above the bridge and the Captain's cabin. I don't remember it being a balmy night. Still, we were alcohol-fuelled and acting barmy as we turned up the tunes and danced away on the upper deck.

Unfortunately, the Captain had a different taste in music and did not appreciate us tap dancing above his bedroom on a metal deck. So, at 2 am, the question had to be asked, and the decision had to be made. "Where are you sleeping then, girls?" asked Andy. We waited expectantly. This was one time when I couldn't be a loser, whatever the answer. There was no need to take one for the team this time. "We are going to camp on the hill," they replied. While being surprised, we considered it a stalling option until they discussed and decided which of us they were settling for. I chipped back this time. "Don't be silly, girls. It's too late to put tents up. You can stay on board. We both have our own cabins." "No, we don't want to put you out at all. We are happy to camp," they came back at us. This was getting difficult, so we changed tack slightly to get some movement. "Just come and look at the cabins and nice accommodation you can have instead of a windy tent," I said as I led them down the two levels to the cabins near the bar.

    Andy's cabin was next to mine, and we showed them both through the door of each for comparison purposes. The deal is almost done, we were thinking. Then just when we thought it was all over, Andy scored an own goal with the comment, "look how big the beds are. Plenty of room for two" A master stroke, he was thinking, what will they say now? "So where will you sleep then?" was the reply.

And that's how I found myself sharing a bed top and tail with a six-foot magnum look alike while two hot Swedish girls cuddled up together inches away through the wall. A footnote for history is when asked the question "where will you sleep?" the answer should be "here with you, and Dave next door with your mate", not "well, I will share with Dave if you have this bed."

So, the answer to Barry Island's most famous question, 'What's occurring?' is absolutely nothing.

A FLIGHT OF FANCY

I joined my first shipping company as a very green and wide-eyed cadet. I had just turned seventeen when I started my first year at Southampton Polytechnic. Southampton had long been associated with shipping, especially the old trans-Atlantic passenger liners and more recently, the cruise ships that docked there.

I had chosen Shaw Saville over other shipping companies for three key reasons. The first was that my best friend Dave Gilbert had just joined six months before and handed me the address and instructions for an apprenticeship application. The second reason was that they had a fleet of 32 ships and a well-recognised cadet scheme with good prospects. And finally, they had passenger liners. It was known that P&O and Cunard had tough competition due to the large number of cadets they employed. Shaw

Saville had many fewer, and it was known that the Cadets always got a chance to go on at least one cruise ship. To a seventeen-year-old boy from a small town, that meant one thing, access to women, lots of women.

Alas, in my second year at college, disaster struck before setting foot at sea for the first time when the Company sold its Liners. The pride of the fleet, the Northern Star and Southern Cross Passenger Ships, were sold to the Greeks, who seemed to be trying to buy the whole British merchant fleet in the 70s. So, with a heavy heart after completing my training, I left Shaw Saville with just six remaining ships and joined Fyffes. Yes, that is Fyffes, the banana company, but also the Company that owned the ships, the plantations, and the towns and ports we visited across Central and South America. More importantly, when the rest of the shipping industry was reducing, they had doubled their fleet from six to twelve ships.

I was at home for an extended period waiting for my second ship appointment from

Fyffes when the joining instructions arrived in the post. Knowing that some of their key routes were the UK and Europe to Central America and back, I expected a train ticket to Avonmouth. However, I got a total surprise when I opened the letter. It was such a surprise that I whooped with excitement. The letter informed me that I was to join the MV Darien in Singapore. This was a dream come true for me. I had never managed to make it to the Far East, and Singapore had a particular attraction to me.

I busied myself getting ready for a long-haul flight. This involved searching the house for a case worthy of an international traveller and capable of surviving a long-haul trip with British Airways. Then without warning, I got another letter two days later that told me it was all cancelled and to wait for further instructions.

The level of disappointment I felt was not balanced by the possibility of extra time at home. When my official leave had run out and I was waiting for a ship, it was effectively additional free holidays, but relaxing and enjoying them was impossible. I had to be available to join a ship within 24 hours notice, so I could only plan one day at a time. No long-term projects could be started, such as stripping down my car or painting the outside of mum's house. In those days before mobile phones and instant communications, holidays or any long-distance travel were also difficult, if not impossible, whilst waiting for an appointment letter. I sat at home dejected and awaited the train ticket to Avonmouth within every post for the next week. It was another 40 years before I eventually made it to Singapore.

Eventually, a letter arrived and I could tell by the envelope and franking it was from the Company. I opened it with disappointment already building inside me, which turned into disbelief as I saw the instructions. Fly from Heathrow at 10.30 pm on Tuesday and arrive at Hobart, Tasmania, at 5.30 pm on Thursday. I was excited all over again, although I wasn't even sure where

Tasmania was. I just knew it was a long way and somewhere near Australia. My little knowledge of Tasmania came from the Tasmanian Devil Looney Tunes Cartoons, in which Taz was generally portrayed as living in a jungle. Without the benefit of internet access, the only accurate source of information was the library, so I set off immediately to the local offering in Corringham town centre.

The one-room small-town library was limited in its capacity, and I had lost my library card many years ago. Luckily there was a reference and travel section that met my needs. I targeted the atlas section first. Going straight to the world map section looking for the southern hemisphere and the Far East in particular. My gut feeling was fifty percent correct in that it was near Australia. Still, I did not expect it to be south of Australia, and I certainly did not know it belonged to Australia. I did know that flying long haul meant I needed to upgrade my old suitcase, and it was time to go shopping.

Five days later, I was sitting in the departure lounge at Heathrow with the heaviest hand luggage I could get through baggage allowance. Even though we had a generous weight allowance of 30kg, it was always difficult to pack for a trip of four to six months. In the days before microelectronics, everything was heavy. Your stereo cassette player alone could fill a large part of your case, plus all those cassette tapes to last six months. Thus, all the heavy items like steel toecap boots and tools would always be in hand baggage, which usually went through without being weighed.

Unfortunately for Mac, the engineer cadet flying with us, this was not the usual short-haul flight. I met Mac at the check-in desk. I knew there were seven of us flying to the ship, but being new to the Company, I did not know any of them. Fortunately, Fyffes provided all staff with stickers for their cases to easily identify them. I could see one on the case next to me at check-in. It was a round sticker with Fyffes line written around the edge and their newest ship steaming at speed in the centre.

"Are you joining a ship?" I asked him. "Yes, the Darien, and you?" "Yes, me too," I replied, "pretty cool to be flying to Australia, isn't it?" "Well, it was until they put my hand baggage on the scale." He said. He was busy digging into his bag to remove heavy items as we talked. There was a total weight allowance for all bags on long-haul flights, and he had gone over by 4kg. "Can you pay excess baggage to put it through?" I asked. "Yes," he replied, "but it's charged by the distance, and this will cost me £65." That was a fortune to us both at the time. I was joining as a junior engineer and was earning at least twice his wage, which I believe must have been around £110 a month at the time.

"Let me check in, and I will help you," I responded. I wasn't sure how I could help and was now one person away from the check-in scales that had caused this chaos.

I hoped I would not be in the same situation, and the bag on my shoulder felt heavier by the second. Eventually, I placed my case gingerly on the scale. This was my new Samsonite case that had cost the equivalent of a month's wages for Mac. It was a huge case, one of the first on the market with wheels and a retractable handle, which I thought were marvellous.

"Ok, can you put your hand luggage on the scale as well, please?" said the British Airways check-in Clerk. I placed the bag on the scale very slowly and gently, hoping this would somehow register a lower weight despite my knowledge of the laws of physics telling me otherwise. The bright red digital numbers flickered briefly and then settled down. "That's ok, Mr Houghton," she said, "you may take your hand baggage off now." I breathed a sigh of relief and immediately looked across to Mac, sitting on his case nearby, as he gave me a weak smile and a thumbs up.

I walked over, pleased but trying not to look so in front of Mac and his problem. "So, what are you going to do about the weight?"

I said. "Already done it", he responded as he held up the crossed fingers on his right hand "just waiting to get re-weighed". The person at the check-in desk moved on. Mac jumped in to throw his bags back on the scale with begrudging looks from those in the queue behind. Whatever he had done was successful, and his bags were cleared to fly. And that is how Mac joined a ship without the two engineering essentials for going to sea, his boiler suits and steel toecap engine room boots. But fear not; he still had his Ghetto Blaster, cassettes, and essential 'private' reading material.

As we sat in the departure lounge, we discussed the others who would be joining us and scanned the room for likely seafarers. We had plenty of time and opportunity to engage in one of my favourite pastimes of people-watching. There were some starting points to help us in our 'spot a seafarer' search.

The first was that we were probably looking for men. Although I had sailed with female deck cadets, they were the exception to the rule, and the industry was still overwhelmingly male-orientated.

The age range was flexible but likely to be in the area of eighteen to thirty. This is the range before family ties, and the need to change careers before it's too late meant many left the industry to work ashore. Those that didn't make the step by then would likely be at sea for their whole career because they get used to the wages, lifestyle, and position. After thirty, it was often too late to start again in a new direction, possibly much nearer the bottom of the career and wages ladder.

Next, they would be travelling alone and carrying oversized hand baggage that looked heavy, possibly with a large stereo or Ghetto Blaster on view. Finally, they would be some of the saddest faces in the room. Whilst the rest of the passengers were flying to holidays, relatives, or even a brief business trip, we were flying away from home. Not just away but away to work seven days a week for the next four to six months. We had little to smile about.

Mac and I spotted our first target, and he probably spotted us too as he walked across the lounge and took a seat just one away from me. I leaned across to open the conversation. "Are you joining a ship?" I asked.

"Yes", was the reply. I cheered internally at my powers of observation and deduction. Watch and learn Sherlock Holmes, I thought. Then he continued with the ship's name, and Mac and I looked at each other in confusion.

"So, you are not joining the MV Darien with Fyffes?" I asked.

"No, I work for BP. I am flying to Dubai", was his surprising response.

We introduced ourselves as fellow seafarers and explained that we had spotted him. He explained that he had thought the same and sat nearby to check his suspicions. Much mutual back-slapping later, we were now a team of three scanning the lounge for more victims.

Then we spotted him, mid-twenties carrying too much, looking confused, unhappy, and seeking solace anywhere. He desperately needed a friendly face to talk to. We sat and waited for our moment, and he eventually looked across in our direction. As I caught his eye, I raised my eyebrows to say, hi, we have seen you. Do you want to engage? He raised his head in acknowledgement and turned his body in our direction with a nervous step toward us. "Are you joining a ship?" I asked.

"Yes," he said, "I am so glad to see you here".

"Fyffes Line?" I said quickly to avoid the same mistake again.

"Darien", he responded. "Hello, I'm Phil Cheeseborough, Electrician", he continued. We all introduced ourselves and settled back to spot the next victim. We only found one more in the lounge but managed to spot two more on the plane, and eventually, all seven of us got together for a beer at our first stop in Dubai.

Phil and I made our first connection in Dubai over a beer, a tradition that would continue for several years. Phil and I became good mates working on several ships together over the next few years. That friendship was often cemented by the fact that we were always the last to leave the bar. We were generally the first to get there too, and together, we managed the bars on most ships we were on. We liked our beer cold and plentiful and could never rely on others to ensure it was stocked and cooled in time.

As we took a break in the lounge, at Dubai, during re-fuelling, Phil saw the bar and went straight to it for seven beers. Seven cold lagers were duly poured and making their way to our table. As I returned to carry the last two, Phil looked at me in shock. "Have you got cash on you?" he asked.

"Yes, but just pounds, nothing foreign". I replied. This was 1980, debit cards hadn't been invented, and credit cards were not always as acceptable around the world as they are today.

"Sterling is fine," he said. "I just don't have enough for the round".

"What, you haven't brought cash to travel across the world?" I responded.

"Yes, but I didn't expect to pay forty pounds for seven beers" to put this into perspective, a pint of beer at home was as low as 40p, and this round would have been less than £5 even in central London. I handed Phil £20, and we sat down to enjoy our drinks and cement our long-term drinking partnership with the most expensive beer we had ever bought.

In truth, my friendship with Phil had already gotten off to a very friendly start on the plane itself. Check-in had placed the seven of us in seats close to each other. Phil was sitting next to me on my right, and it was soon clear why he was looking for a friendly face at the airport. He was terrified of flying and about to set off on a long-haul flight to Australia for the next day and a half. I had the window seat, which Phil was grateful for as he constantly fiddled with his seat belt and asked me what was happening and why it took so long. Like many who fear flying, the real problem is taking off and landing, not the flying itself. As long as there is no turbulence.

I was about to find out that was very true for Phil. As we taxied down the runway, he grabbed the arm of the seat and squeezed. The fact that my hand was already on the arm did not occur to him initially. Still, as we hit take-off speed and left the ground, we discussed that he was squeezing all the blood from my fingers and just squeezed harder. Despite the discomfort, I was not going to move my hand. I could see the genuine fear in his eyes and he needed that human contact. Basically, it was a hand to hold as you would with a girlfriend or children, but men don't do that, do they? So, this was as close as it could get, and it became the norm for every take-off and landing, all the way to Hobart.

At the beginning of our journey, as we had waited at Heathrow for our take-off slot, the plane in front was a Qantas Jumbo. It was also here in Dubai and soon became a regular sight. We were in a British Airways Jumbo and followed each other across the world to Sydney. Thanks to this duplication, both flights were underutilised, and our plane was only about 25% full, giving each of us whole rows of 4 seats to stretch across. It was a luxury I had never experienced before and have never experienced since. It also meant we did manage to get some sleep, and Phil could relax between the regular bone-crushing sessions of take-offs and landings.

Finally, after multiple breakfasts and dinners, on board, and a two-hour interconnecting flight from Sydney, we eventually arrived in Hobart on Thursday at 5.30 pm. It was early evening when we booked into the hotel in the centre of Hobart. We agreed to shower, change and meet in the bar. As we gathered in the bar, it was clear that travelling had taken its toll on all of us. Despite the excitement of being in Australia, the conversation was subdued, and we struggled to find the energy to engage in any meaningful way.

Nevertheless, I was keen to see the city before we left early in the morning to join the ship. The group was less than enthusiastic. "Surely this is a chance to see Hobart," I said, "we will probably never be here again, and it is just outside the door". There was a mumble of conversation about bed and sleeping before two voices piped up to agree with me. One was Phil, and the other was Andy. Andy Thompson was the other junior engineer joining the ship with me and was also new to the company. He was destined to become a close friend; eventually, we were each other's best men. So, Phil, Andy, and I set off in search of adventure and nightlife.

The first bar was quiet, and after one beer, we set off again to find more excitement. As we sat in the second bar, the tiredness hit us like a wave. This bar was also quiet, and a chat with the bar staff indicated that we were not quite in the centre of town and it was Thursday, so most of the city would be quiet until tomorrow night. We had not even considered this. In all honesty, we were no longer sure what day of the week it was, and we didn't really care. I felt my eyes close several times before I was challenged from across the table.

I woke in time to witness Phil and Andy dropping off and waking with a rapid lift of their head and the sudden realisation that they were in a public place. Reluctantly we all agreed that we were too tired to continue, and the call from our beds was just too strong to resist any longer. We persuaded ourselves that we were missing nothing and that there was probably nothing to see in the city of Hobart.

We will never know if we were right or whether the best nightlife and party was happening in a stunning historic architectural wonder just around the corner. We didn't care. We knew where our beds were, and there was plenty of Tasmania we had yet to discover.

Back at my hotel room, I prepared for an early morning exit. I packed and closed my new indestructible Samsonite case and dragged it to the door, with its now bent and non-retracting handle thanks to one flight on British Airways.

DON'T TRY THIS AT HOME

Being woken up early in Hobart after a two-day flight from Heathrow was not a highlight of the trip. Seven of us were joining M.V. Darien at Port Huon in Tasmania.

There was no excitement around the breakfast table that morning. Instead, the overwhelming emotion was exhaustion. The thrill of flying halfway around the world had utterly dissipated as we trudged our heavy luggage across the hotel lobby and into the waiting minibus.

It was early May 1980, and as we went outside, we did not know what to expect from the weather. Australia was always portrayed as hot and sunny, but this was Tasmania, an island at the southern tip of the Australian mainland and it was autumn down here. As we boarded the minibus, it was apparent that our travelling clothes were suitable for the climate, which was like a late English summer day.

The drive of just over an hour took us high into the hills around Hobart and down the other side towards Port Huon. As we viewed the scenery and chatted with the driver, it dawned on us why the climate felt so familiar. All around us were plantations of apple trees, and that is why the ship was in Port Huon loading a cargo of 'English' Cox's apples. These grew in abundance because of the typically British climate but with a little more warmth, precisely what most of us Brits would aspire to.

Port Huon looked very little like a regular port. It was simply a jetty and a few buildings nearby. There were no fences, gates, signage or control measures, just a ship on a jetty. In many ways, it was smaller than a Central American banana port. At least they have the town next to them to give them context. At first glance, this place just seemed isolated. But we were to discover that civilisation was close in the form of a small town and a Pub.

We found this out as we took handover of our individual jobs from those we were replacing and were flying home the next day. The minibus was waiting to take them back to Hobart, so the handover was brief. It consisted, as always, of the technical stuff, what fails, how to fix it, where to find that special thing to hit it with, as well as the social stuff. This consisted of who was who, the best socialiser, best engineer, best mate, how good the food was, the local bars, and in this extraordinary instance, the keys to a car owned by the local landlord.

It turned out that the local pub was just a couple of miles away. So, for several nights the lads had been frequenting the establishment until the early hours of the morning. Then as they left and were all completely drunk, the landlord handed them the keys to his car and said to bring it back tomorrow. So, they did every day and so did we for the two days we were there. All without a dent or accident, but more by good luck than judgement. Also, and very importantly, with no interest from the local constabulary. So clearly, the lesson is don't try this at home folks.

At this local pub on the first evening, I was introduced to the 1980 version of Australian etiquette. The bar was busy, and an attractive lady was standing in the aisle, leaning over a table and talking to others seated. I had already navigated to the bar and back via the other side of the table. Still, one Aussie man didn't like wasting time getting to the bar. He walked up to her and slapped her full whack across the backside, shouting, "move your frigging arse, Sheila". I expected some verbal retaliation or challenge from her or at least the gents on the table, but not a word was said. She did as requested and simply moved her arse to let Crocodile Dundee get to the bar. Maybe she knew him intimately and her name really was Sheila, but neither seemed likely at the time. I think it is worth repeating, don't try this at home folks.

From the drunk driving, sexist but marvellously welcoming Port Huon, we sailed around the island from south to north coast and the absolutely perfectly named Beauty Point. This was a berth right next to town and a range of bars. Some with views out across the beautiful open bay in all directions where a beer could become a spiritual experience as we sat looking out upon nature. Almost spiritual but not quite, as Andy and I were too busy looking for Tasmanian Devils in the jungle. The jungle in question was more of a dense forest around the town, easily accessible by those too stupid to know better. Beer fuelled discussions with local bar staff confirmed that Tasmanian Devils could be found in the wild, but we were unlikely to see one. However, the Wallabies were much easier to find. So, one lunchtime, we set off into the bush to find a Wallaby. After an hour of fruitless searching and much getting lost, we retreated to town defeated and deflated.

Keen to drown our sorrows, we confided in the next poor barman that served us. After he had stopped laughing, and before saying anything, he pointed to the pin board across the bar, which had a range of photos alongside the football and dart team fixture dates. That's where you will find them, he said. We looked in confusion at the photos, mainly poorly focused images of drunk people and pot-bellied footballers. "Look at the left-hand side," he said. That's my daughter and her friends at school". As we looked closer, there was a group of children leaning through the fence of a school playground. The photo was taken from outside the fence to capture the view to the best effect. "I took that last year when she first started school. She told me it happens every dinner time. So, I went to see, and it does, every day".

The photo showed a group of young schoolchildren thrusting their hands and lunches through the bars of the school railings to feed a mob of Wallabies on the other side. The barman continued. "Wallabies are like rats or pigeons round here. They have become so used to us, so if you want to see one, you go into town, not the bush, especially at dinner time".

Realising we were never going to Challenge David Attenborough, we abandoned our wildlife career and reverted to type. We ordered another beer, raised our glasses to the photo and declared that we did see a Wallaby in Tasmania after all.

THE ORIGIN OF SPECIES
(Marinus enginus merchantica)

It was not unusual for me to buy my Christmas cards in Woolworths, but I had never paid in New Zealand dollars before. It was December 18th 1976, and the culmination of a journey that had taken a month at sea but, in reality, had started many years before.

I had spent the previous two years studying marine engineering at Southampton Polytechnic, but my introduction to seafaring was at the age of seven as I watched the launch of the M.V. Scythia at Cammell Laird in Birkenhead. My dad had been a Second engineer in Cunard for many years. That meant he spent a long time away from home, but I knew little about what his job involved until I stood next to him on the launch platform that day. Dad was going to be the Chief Engineer for the maiden voyage and as we stood with the VIPs above a cheering crowd, I thought he must be really important and very clever to take this massive vessel across the sea.

A year later, I was equally impressed when I stayed on board for a few days in the Royal Albert Dock in London. Little was I to know at the age of seven that ten years later, I would be in the Shaw Savill offices at the end of the same dock signing my Cadet indenture papers.

I had never desired or sought to be a seafarer when I left school. I just knew that I wanted to get away from the town of Stanford-le-hope. It was not a bad place to live, but to a teenager, it felt like a one-horse town. The population of 15,000 lived there mainly to commute to work in central London. I witnessed the faces of those travellers on daily train journeys and knew that it was not a future I wanted, although we had moved there for that exact reason in 1967. Dad had left Cunard and got a job with Pfizer in Poplar and travelled an hour and a half each way every day for five years until eventually getting a job with Powell Duffryn much closer to home.

I found myself leaning towards engineering, particularly the RAF, until my best friend Dave Gilbert joined Shaw Savill and passed on the telephone number. It may not have been my initial desire, but maybe it was my destiny to be a seafarer because I made the phone call, and the rest is history.

One week after that commitment to my marine engineering apprenticeship, I received my acceptance as an RAF mechanic apprentice. Too little too late, but I never regretted choosing the sea over the air.

The connection with the Royal Albert Dock continued right up to my first trip to sea. Having joined S.S Hardwicke Grange in Sheerness at the mouth of the Thames, we then sailed up river into the heart of London and spent three weeks in the Royal Albert Dock. The whole area is now unrecognisable, with the old warehouses being replaced by the Excel Arena and the centre of the dock acting as the runway for London City Airport. The transformation is startling and must be considered an improvement on the old docklands, but when working-class terraced houses are replaced with million-pound flats and fancy Hotels, it does feel a little bit like social cleansing.

Forty years later, I stayed in a hotel on the dock with my family. It was from that dock on 17th November 1976 that we set sail bound for Wellington, and my seafaring career began.

In all honesty, I was a little disappointed to be buying my Christmas cards in Woolworths. After the excitement of sailing halfway around the world, I expected New Zealand to be more exotic and foreign but it was more like a British high street with dollars and funny accents. However, it was not long before I fell in love with New Zealand. In a time before the internet, Sky TV, and cheap air travel, New Zealand was in a time zone of its own. It felt like it was twenty years behind the UK but in a good way. There was no urgency or need to catch up. It was doing fine all by itself, with a small population of 3 million people and 56 million sheep outnumbering them 18:1. The pace of life was slow, and the people chilled.

The climate was very much like the UK but just a bit better. Without the gulf stream affecting its seasons, each was predictable and all a little milder. In the summer, you could plan for sunshine and warm weather, which meant that all sports, but mainly water sports were very popular. This was best demonstrated when we arrived in Bluff at the tip of the South Island on January 17th. Bluff was a small town and ferry terminal at the southern tip of New Zealand and was often referred to as an island, although it was a peninsular connected by a narrow strip of land. It had a population of just 2000, one pub and a drab seaman's mission. I had heard Shaw Savill regulars and even New Zealanders refer to it as the arsehole of the world, but clearly, they had never been to Sheerness. That all changed one sunny Sunday in February 1977.

It was peak summertime with bright sunshine and temperatures up to 30c. The weather had brought the whole population out into the harbour for the annual regatta. We had heard of this via the seaman's mission, invited ourselves in and planned our own unique participation. The Hardwicke Grange was a Shaw Savill experiment for cadet training, and there were fifteen of us on board. The whole group of us had suffered two months of banter from Officers and Crew alike baiting the first trip greenhorns. Then, to take it further, the crew challenged us to a lifeboat race. We duly accepted the challenge, which was set to take place during the regatta in front of the whole town.

I must point out that lifeboats are designed to get as many people in as possible. They are wide heavy, ungainly and not designed for speed or manoeuvrability. The crew were the ones with the most experience as they often lowered and tested the lifeboats in port but nearly always used the engine. They viewed us as the tortoise and themselves as the hare but without the positive outcome for the tortoise this time. We had different ideas and went into training immediately. This consisted of lowering a lifeboat and rowing it around for an hour to see who would be our best team. Amazingly although I was the smallest and lightest of the group, my rowing technique was good enough to get me selected for the eight-man team.

The big day came, and we rowed the boats around to the regatta start line as the opening race of the event. I think that was in order to get us crazy brits out of the way for the real sailing events to take place. From the start line under the bridge around the end of the jetty and back, a simple straight-line course. Well, it was for our team. We shot away, pulling in unison like a team that had trained for months, not minutes. Within a few minutes, we had not just taken the lead but left them two lengths behind. That soon became three, four and even more as we headed for the turning point. We reached the turn in ten minutes and looked back to see the crew boat in disarray a quarter of the course behind us: As we rowed back and past them, their oars were all out of sync, and their cox had almost given up trying to regain any control over the pantomime happening in front of him.

Things only got worse at the turning point when they veered off in the wrong direction and seemed incapable of getting it back online to the finish. Our race was completed in 20 minutes, and the crew finished almost 10 minutes behind. Embarrassed and beaten, they duly handed over our winnings of a case of beer which was just the icing on the cake of a well-earned revenge.

Basking in our victory, we joined the locals and watched the regatta. In particular, we watched the small dingy class race. Our interest was less in the race than in the participants themselves, a high proportion of which were young, scantily clad females. The winner of the small dingy class was a stunning petite young girl who walked out of the water with a wet T-shirt and the smallest shorts I had ever seen. She threw her long curly hair back like a Loreal advert, and every blue-blooded male gasped involuntarily. I can't remember how I ended up talking to her. I was a very green nineteen-year-old unlikely to make a direct approach, but somehow, we were introduced and we found ourselves on a date the following day, much to the angst of the other cadets.

Bluff was suddenly a very interesting place, although our first date didn't even take place there. We went to the cinema, and the nearest was sixteen miles away in Invercargill. She picked me up in her dad's car. This was a white Triumph 2000, which was his pride and joy, apart from his daughter. Given the high cost of cars in New Zealand and the need to import many of them, this was considered to be the Rolls Royce of Bluff, and it underlined his status as

Chief Engineer of the meat works, which was the biggest employer in the area. It was highly polished and treated with reverence which made it even more surprising that she didn't lock it when we parked at the cinema.

Invercargill was a much bigger town with a population of nearly 50,000. Yet, she walked away from the car, explaining to me that it would never get stolen because that didn't happen there, and anyway, they all knew whom it belonged to and it would be very traceable. At that moment, I realised that being twenty years behind the UK was a good thing, and I wonder if, in the more remote parts of New Zealand, they have managed to maintain that age of innocence to the present day.

My normal routine of pubs and drinking was not possible as she was still only 17 and not yet of legal drinking age. This led to the unusual scenario of our second date being a meal at home with her parents. It was surprisingly pleasant, and much of the conversation was about his beloved car rather than his daughter.

Having satisfied himself that I was a safe and reliable young man to look after his car, he then invited all the cadets and me on a tour of the meat works. This turned into a day out for most of the ship as well as the cadets. The reason the ship was in Bluff was to load frozen lamb so you could consider it as a relevant part of our education, but for any vegetarians amongst you, I will not go into any detail about the day.

Bluff had other unusual attractions too. The most obvious was that Bluff was the biggest supplier of high-quality oysters in New Zealand. Oysters were everywhere in abundance and always turning up on the ship's menus when in Bluff. I tried but failed to eat one from the shell on many occasions, but pouring a dollop of snot down my throat never appealed to me. Nevertheless, I can say I have eaten one. They are so plentiful in Bluff that they were sold in chip shops like chicken nuggets: three deep-fried battered oysters and a portion of chips. I managed to eat one. They may be a celebrated delicacy, but when deep fried, they become a chewy rubber ball with no flavour other than the batter they are in. An experience I never repeated.

My final memory of Bluff was a total surprise following a walk in the bush. With so few drinking establishments, we resorted to walking and sightseeing instead, or maybe I should say in desperation. Unfortunately, one stroll got a little out of hand as we wandered into some dense undergrowth heading for a view of the beach and the sea. After two hours of being lost and battered by undergrowth, we were starting to feel desperate when we eventually broke out of the thicket and onto a small beach with rocky outcrops at the rear of the beach.

Our pleasure at being out of the bush soon turned into complete exuberance and delight as a penguin popped out of a small outcrop. It was small, about a foot tall and just as surprised to see us as we were. A few seconds later, there was another and then, eventually, a small group checking us out from a distance. We kept a safe distance of about 5m away so as not to scare them, and thinking they were babies, we thought they might be hungry. Embarrassingly the only food we had was a bar of Cadbury caramel, and we placed it on a rock in front of them and backed off to let them approach. They did approach but, upon investigation, decided it was not fishy enough.

Following our David Attenborough experience, we discovered that they were most likely to be fully grown adults called small blue penguins visiting from a colony on Stewart Island. For the record, I suspect David Attenborough has omitted this in his research, but now we can confirm that penguins don't eat chocolate.

If you want to see penguins in Bluff, I recommend good walking boots, a survival kit and a machete to reach the beach. Alternatively, you could approach from the other direction within 50 metres of the penguins and find the main road, car park and bus stop that sensible people use.

I visited my New Zealand crush on my next trip, and we exchanged letters for over a year. I am ashamed to admit I can no longer remember her name, but the sight of her walking out of the water in those tight white shorts is forever embedded in my memory bank. So, Bluff may not be the arsehole of the world, but if you say Bluff, I still think arse.

CRAZY FROG

"Run" was the shout. And I did, without question or reason. I did not know who shouted the command, but I knew it felt right, and there was no time to discuss the situation.

I had already seen the jeep coming up the steep jungle track through the foliage in front of us. From the speed they were travelling and the raised voices on board, they were not coming here to join us for a social drink at the Picnic Bar.

As we stumbled through the greenery before us, it got denser with every step. It was whipping and cutting into our bare legs below the shorts and the forearms we held up to protect our faces. It was only just taller than us, so although it was not a thick rainforest, it was certainly not a walk in the park. The slope of the hill was also something we should have expected.

As we sat at the table near the short wall looking down the hill, we could see it was steep. We had walked the mile up the track to get here, but this was very much a short, direct route down, and the slope could not be tackled at running speed. I remember a brief thought crossed my mind about what animals I might encounter before we got out of this vegetation. The fact that this whole episode started with a large jungle frog reminded me that snakes eat frogs, and larger jungle animals eat snakes. Not to mention the smaller insects and spiders at the lower end of the food chain for the frog itself.

The thought was brief as my mind recalled the view of the jeep with four khaki policemen with guns clearly looking to enforce their authority regardless of blame. Tales of breaking knuckles with a gun butt as a starting point kept us running headlong into unknown dangers to escape the known risk of aggressive policing for minor crimes. We hadn't even committed a crime unless you call making a barman angry a crime. Surely it was totally unfair of him to call the police after we had probably doubled his weekly income in a single two-hour afternoon session. In an attempt to drink his fridge dry, we had been drinking cans in the glorious Costa Rican afternoon sunshine as we looked across the jungle over the view of Golfito harbour. As the beers went down, the beer can pyramid went up, carefully balanced on the low-level rough concrete wall that separated us from the jungle. All appeared to be going well until we spotted the frog.

The frog was huge and had an attitude. It sat in the jungle plants less than 10 feet away and made enough noise to stop the four of us talking. It was as big as a dinner plate and as loud as a foghorn. It appeared to deliberately interrupt our conversation every time we attempted to talk. I swear it knew precisely what it was doing. At this stage, the alcohol overcame our common sense, and someone had the good idea to chase it away by throwing a beer can at it. One became two and three, and the barman suddenly expressed displeasure at this blatant littering around his bar.

We ceased, but we were now in fits of uncontrollable laughter. Engaged in conversation with a large green amphibian whilst simultaneously arguing with the barman as the massive pyramid of cans started to clatter in all directions into the bar and jungle. The noise and chaos eventually caused the frog to hop away, happy that he had won. Meanwhile, the barman waved the phone at us, telling us the police were on the way. That was definitely our cue to leave.

Finally, we were near the bottom of the hill, and as we broke out into the sunshine, we were directly onto the corner of the main street and the path back up to the bar. We carried on walking to the ship at a steady pace. We didn't hang around in case the police had decided to come chasing us, as we certainly wouldn't be hard to identify. Some local children looked at us, somewhat bedraggled and red all over from the heat exertion and the constant thrashing with plants during our great escape. They shouted something in Spanish that was undoubtedly not complimentary. Then, they wandered off laughing at the crazy sailors who dared to go into the jungle in flip-flops and t-shirts.

They clearly didn't know about the crazy frog that had driven us there. Crazy frog, now there's an idea!

LAND OF MILK AND HONEY

I woke through a blurred fog of confusion. I was in bed or, more accurately, on a bed because I felt exposed. Not cold, but I didn't feel covered. As I slowly started to open my eyes, I reached out to find a light sheet on top of me, and as my vision cleared, I found myself looking up at a blank white ceiling. That was not unusual, but the six-foot wide, slowly rotating fan blades were certainly not normally above my bed.

Whilst the fan itself was unusual, its movement was more of a concern to me. It was rotating just slowly enough to follow it with my eyes. It was not the rotation that worried me, more the horizontal movement as the blades swayed up and down like a mad axe man scything through a forest. Whilst the engineer in me visually checked out the central mountings for security, the man in me detected something soft and delicate against my thigh. As I looked to my right, I was surprised to find my company was a young slim and very attractive lady wearing nothing but the sheet that we shared between us.

My mind was racing now. The first thought was about the lovely lady next to me, but that was quickly overtaken by thoughts of where was I and more importantly, where should I be? This was quickly followed by where were all my mates that were going to stay together and ensure we all got back to the ship safely?

The thoughts started to form slowly. Walking into town, stopping at the first decent bar with music playing, only to find the whole crew already there. Then the Captain and Chief Engineer arrived to join the throng. I remember lots of rum and dancing with the lady, who was now lying next to me.

My thoughts turned back to her. How could I help it? She was lovely. She looked to be in her early twenties with olive skin and unusually fair hair for this part of the world. I had been to Columbia often but always just banana ports, sometimes even without a jetty and bananas loaded off barges whilst the ship stayed at anchor. This was different and a great treat to be in a proper port in Santa Marta, Colombia. Apart from a few brief contacts with boatmen, this was my first real opportunity to meet real Colombians. It had gone well. I remember a night of drinking and dancing with a genuine party atmosphere with the girls, but I did not plan or expect to be here in the morning.

As I looked at her, she woke up and smiled, saying good morning in Spanish, which sounded so sexy compared with English. We exchanged some pigeon English and Spanish pleasantries, and she was clearly asking if I was going as she curled back into sleep. I found a clock with the time and realised I needed to leave. I asked if I could kiss her, which seemed strange considering what we had been up to a few hours before. I kissed her cheek and left with her softness and smell still lingering in my thoughts.

I left her in bed with the fan swinging over her like some James Bond film plot waiting to happen. I gathered pace down the narrow staircase partly because I needed to hurry and partly because they were surprisingly steep and curved at the bottom to spit you out into a blank white hallway below. I was met with a conundrum of doors in all directions. I believed I knew the way out from the strength of the sun at the end of the hall, but I just wanted one peek through the door to my right. I was correct. Here was the bar from the night before. Smaller than I remembered but well-appointed for a bar in Central America, the beer was cold too, until the fateful decision was taken to start drinking Cuba Libres. That, I thought, is why I ended up staying the night. I must keep off the rum. It makes me reckless.

I had caught sight of the clock in the bar and was concerned that either time had moved quickly or her clock upstairs was slow. It was now 6.20 am. I never wore a watch ashore in Central or South American countries as it attracted muggers. It was a simple but logical philosophy. No watches, no cameras, no show of wealth, and keep $10 in your sock to get home. It worked for me for ten years at sea, and I always got back safe, even when alone. First, however, I needed to find the ship and get back. It was due to sail at 7 am, and I was the engineering watchkeeper to take her out.

I opened the door onto the street and was hit by the brightest penetrating light I had seen. It was like the sun was aiming specifically at me for that moment. Even at this time of the morning, it was warm but not yet uncomfortably so, which was a good job because I could see the dock in the distance. A very long way in the distance. The walk the night before had seemed short, but looking now, the port looked at least 2 miles away. The $10 in my sock was lost, as it often was on a night out. Most commonly, it was due to a swim on the way back down the beach, which would result in losing it from your sock and being picked up off the beach by local children. I liked to think that this was a way of helping them out. They would certainly take it back to the family and be a substantial bonus for them to feed and care for the children.

Today the sock money was irrelevant as I actually had money in my pocket. This was unusual on a night out as I usually took what I could afford to spend or lose and no more. However, this was also irrelevant as there were no taxis I could see, so I started to jog in the general direction of the docks.

The jog turned into a run as panic kicked in, and then back to a walk as the alcohol from the night before started to slow me down. As I passed the dock gates, I was genuinely concerned that the ship was still far into the docks and might sail without me. Then my guardian angel turned up. Not with a halo and wings but with a milk float. An actual, very English-looking, electric milk float full of crates. I gave the driver a nod and pointed before jumping on the back to ride in the ship's direction. Even better, it soon became apparent that it was going to deliver to the ship. So, it looked like I would be on time after all. I could get on board straight down to the engine room, and nobody would be any the wiser. No lateness, no awkward questions.

The milk float stopped at the ship, and I jumped off as it pulled to a halt. Feeling a new lease of life and success, I skipped up the gangway two steps at a time, eager to get my feet on deck and say I have arrived. I felt smug as my foot hit the deck, and I headed straight off to the engine room entrance when I heard a voice behind me. Good morning, Dave, nice night.

I gasped and slumped physically as I saw the Chief and Captain leaning on the rail. They had seen my arrival by milk float, and my run of joy was now the walk of shame. Before I could reply, the chief said 7 am on the spot, just on time. It was a vote of confidence to say you're ok, it's fine, go do your job now. Then just for good measure, the Captain chipped in with we are sailing at nine, which told me you have two hours to get it ready and make the most of it.

I was lucky this time, it was a close call, but there will be others, and that's the fun of it.

SWIMMING WITH THE FISHES

Tela in Honduras was always one of the favourite banana ports to visit. It was the simplicity of its layout, its people and its culture.

Welcoming and accommodating, the people always had a smile for you, and it had everything you needed within a short walk of the ship. The town was a long thin strip stretching along a beautiful sandy beach with a backdrop of palm trees. Centrally located right in the middle of the town was the jetty. This stuck straight out into the sea at a perfect 90-degree angle to the beach. The ship would dock at the far end in the deepest water, and the train line ran straight through the centre of the town and the entire length of the jetty. The jetty was a simple wooden structure with no buildings, making it non-industrial and keeping with the simple beauty of the town and its surroundings.

From the end of the jetty, a left turn would take you into town with bars and shops whilst a right turn took you along an area of housing, and tucked in amongst them was a hotel with a swimming pool. This was a real rarity in banana ports and a little bit of luxury with its bar and restaurant.

Luxury was nice, but the real Tela was to be found left of the jetty amongst the bars and the locals. The drink, as always, was locally made rum, usually served as Cuba Libre and always exceptionally strong. Tela was no more affluent than other banana ports but felt less poor. Despite this, some families lived in shacks made of boxes on the beach, and kids fished with bent pins and pieces of banana. Incredibly they actually caught fish with banana bait. Whichever direction you went in Tela, it was a safe bet that you always walked back along the beach. After many local Cuba Libres, a dip in the sea was inevitable. So was the transfer of $10 from your sock to the local children.

Tela also had one of the best challenges to catch out any seafarer who had not been there before. At the end of the jetty was a small bush with tiny red chilli peppers. On the walk into town, the challenge was always to eat a chilli off the bush for $10. I have witnessed this challenge being done just once, and it ended with two crew being violently sick immediately and suffering for many hours afterwards. In a poor town with shacks on the beach and children fishing with bananas, it is common sense that if the locals don't eat them, neither should you.

Unfortunately, we did not heed this lesson when it came to swimming. One of the cadets had brought with him an underwater camera. Commonplace now, but fancy stuff in 1980. The water in Tela was beautifully clear, and the tropical fish we could see were amazing, even from the surface. Thus, we excitedly donned our masks and snorkels and dived off the jetty. The fish on view were fantastic and colourful, but the real aim was to get a photo of us sitting on the propeller.

Although I have never seen the photo as proof, we did achieve our aim and posed on the propeller.

The same evening, we discussed this with the locals when the conversation went strangely quiet. They looked at each other and then responded with a question. "Do you ever see us locals swimming in the sea?" we had to admit the beach was generally empty, with nobody swimming. "Do you not like swimming?" I asked.

"Oh no, we like swimming, but we don't like sharks". Was the response, and that is when I learnt that the locals always know best.

MAN OVERBOARD!

Jimmy was a good tea maker, but it was one of his few skills.

With only two junior engineers on board, I had drawn the short straw and had Jimmy, the greaser, as my seagoing watch assistant. Jimmy had been at sea all his life, and now in his late forties, he had accumulated nearly 30 years of experience. The only problem was that his excessive alcohol consumption had slowly eroded his expertise. He never appeared drunk and incapable, but that was the real problem, as he never appeared sober and fully capable either. He had the look of a man with a history of heavy drinking. His complexion, the look in his eyes, and heavy over-exaggerated movements all highlighted his long-term relationship with alcohol.

Alcoholism was all too familiar for long-term seafarers. With duty-free spirit prices at £1.50 a bottle and nothing to do after work, it was an inevitable hazard of the job not just limited to Jimmy.

Jimmy was capable of the basic watchkeeping duties of checking levels in boilers, cleaning filters and making tea, and he was pleasant enough company. This was our third Atlantic crossing on watch together, and we had got on quite well. But, alas, our partnership did not last the third crossing due to a routine lifeboat drill.

Lifeboat drill was carried out once a week and involved the whole ship's crew regardless of whether you were sleeping between watches. This particular drill took place at 10 am, two hours after finishing our 4-8 am watch. Once the drill alarm was sounded, all crew went to designated posts and the port or starboard muster points. Teams would then practice lowering the boat to deck level before hoisting them back into a secure position again.

When lowered to be level with the deck, it was possible to step across a 12-inch gap and into the boat. Noticing a loose rope hanging over the edge of the starboard lifeboat, the first mate asked Jimmy to step in to retrieve and secure it safely. We were sailing at 18 knots in Caribbean waters on a beautiful sunny day with calm seas and no wind. Jimmy stepped into the boat safely and started gathering the rope, but as he tugged at it, he fell backwards. To my horror, I saw him fall into the tiny gap between the boat and the ship's side. Running to the side, I looked over just as he hit the water.

The lifeboats were positioned midships, so my first fear was that he would be dragged into the ship's side and hit by the propeller. My second fear was that I remembered from one of our conversations that he couldn't swim. This was shocking to me but apparently quite common. I could not understand how anyone could spend weeks crossing vast expanses of water if they could not swim.

The alarm was raised, and the man-overboard procedure was implemented like clockwork. A lifebelt was thrown into the sea, followed by several others with small intervals of time in between. Meanwhile, the captain had initiated a Williamson turn. This manoeuvre put the ship hard to starboard in an effort to keep the propellor away from the casualty, and the ship listed heavily to the port side. I ran straight to the stern of the ship in the hope of spotting Jimmy, and we did see him in the distance, so he had safely missed the propellors but was now a long way from the ship.

My mind was racing now. I knew that anyone falling overboard in the ocean has less than a 25% chance of recovery in ideal conditions. Although our conditions were good, we were in a vast open sea with no landmarks or points of reference. We were also in shark-infested waters. Jimmy was not only fully dressed, complete with heavy steel toecap boots but also couldn't swim. The only thing in his favour was that he was wearing his life jacket for boat drill.

The ship listed heavily to the opposite side as the captain changed course to port. This was to bring the ship around along the line we had been heading. Trusting in the captain's skills, I ran straight to the bow with many of the crew to scan the horizon in all directions. After what seemed like hours but was probably 10 minutes, we saw the first of the lifebelts ahead of us. In the far distance, we could see another and another forming a line to follow to our lost man.

The ship slowed as we looked and listened intently for any sign of Jimmy. Although it was a clear day and the sea was calm, the small waves made it difficult to see anything in the water. The lifebelts would pop into visibility on the top of a wave and then disappear again until rising with the next wave sporadically. We heard Jimmy before we could see him. From the bow, we could hear someone shouting, but the relatively small waves still hid him from our view. The first spot came from the higher vantage point of the bridge and the keen binoculars of the second mate.

We had found him, and he was alive. The relief was overwhelming. The lifeboat was lowered all the way this time and set off to bring in our casualty. As he came back up in the lifeboat and stepped out onto the deck, I greeted him and asked how he survived without swimming. He responded that he had just floated on his back. I said, "but you still have your heavy steel toecap boots on", to which he replied, "Of course, they are new ones. I didn't want to lose them."

I realised then that he didn't truly realise the seriousness of the position he was in but it certainly hit him later. He was put in the hospital room. On a merchant ship, this is little more than a room with a bed, some plasters, antibiotics and very scarily, a Captain's DIY surgery manual. Jimmy went into shock and remained in the hospital until getting off at the first port three days later.

I visited him regularly, and it was hard to tell whether his symptoms were really shock or withdrawal from his daily alcohol fix. Either way, I am glad to say he left us in good health, even if it was just until he found the hotel bar.

OOH LA LA!

"You can't come on board. This is a British territory, and I have command."
The Captain's words rang around the ship's deck as we all cheered in unison at this very British response to our French counterparts.

Not just French counterparts but French Police. The scene was now escalating into farce and resembling the Monty Python sketch from the Holy Grail, with the French taunting the English from the castle. But, in this case, the tide was turned. Our very well-spoken English Captain stood at the top of the gangway, firing a polite broadside across the bows of the French police on the quayside below.

It had all started so well. It was an easy two-mile walk from our usual berth in the harbour to the middle of Le Havre, but the local supermarket was even closer, just a mile away. We knew this from our regular six weekly visits to Le Havre. As soon as we docked, our usual arrival plan of action was implemented in preparation for our evening barbeque with cheese, wine and pâté. The radio officer and off-duty engineer would take the supermarket trolley, from the generator room, to the supermarket in the afternoon. The trolley had been borrowed from this same supermarket two years before. It was now on permanent loan returning to its home shopping trip every six weeks. Having filled it full of baguettes, pate, cheese and wine, we headed back to the ship past the regular bars when we saw that one was well populated with the ship's crew and deck officers.

There was regular banter between engineers and the deck side to throw a challenge in at unsuspecting moments. Challenges would often involve standing on your head or tap dancing. In a pre-politically correct world, it was usually followed by the accusation that they were queer. A strange anomaly even in 1979, as many of our stewards were gay. This was always accepted and embraced by those at sea. Seafarers were always enlightened to race, creed, and all differences in the human form and psyche before the rest of the world eventually caught up. Racism, homophobia or bullying in any form was never accepted, but in a high-pressure job, the banter was an essential survival tool. Although not pleasant to look back on in hindsight,

The trolley was parked outside, and the Fourth Engineer, Radio Officer (adopted as an engineer), and I approached the bar door. The bar was known to us and was long and narrow, running deep from the door with one row of tables to the left and the bar to the right. We threw the door open simultaneously, shouting, "all deck side that can't tap dance are queer". Instantly 70% of the bar stood up. Tables were thrown forwards, and chairs were thrown back, falling as they went. And a dozen fully grown adults started tap dancing for no apparent reason. This was no river dance with disciplined choreography. This was a full-blown, wild inebriated dance with flailing arms and legs everywhere, accompanied by colourful language, whatever your nationality. And in the middle of the mayhem were our two gay stewards tap dancing for all their worth.

The dancing was enough to have the three of us in tears at the door, but the look on the local's faces was the best result. The barman had a massive grin as he understood enough English and knew us well enough to see the joke. Moreover, he could see this would lead to at least another hour of drinking and many beers being sold. The locals, meanwhile, were in a different place altogether. Not understanding our English initially, they were suddenly greeted with their quiet bar full of tap-dancing lunatics and flying chairs. Plus, idiots with trolleys full of wine and bread, pissing themselves with laughter at the door. Their facial expressions alone made the whole event worthwhile.

Thus, the day progressed, beers were drunk, and we eventually returned to the ship for our planned barbeque with our supermarket stash. The barbeque took place on the officer's deck at the rear of the accommodation block. This gave great views of the stern, both sides of the ship, and the gangway down to the quayside. It all started typically. Food was eaten, beer and wine were drunk, and another challenge was thrown out. This first-past-the-post challenge took advantage of the locality and what it had to offer. It offered a line of forklift trucks parked neatly in a row on the quayside but slightly angled towards the ship. To a few drunken racing fans, it looked like a Le Mans start line, and we were in France after all.

So, the challenge was on. Teams of two, one driving and one riding to the end of the jetty, then swap and first past the line on the way back. This was before health and safety ruled the world, so untrained drivers running into docks was not a consideration. Highly likely but not considered. The race was on, and I was an observer on deck as chaos ensued on the dockside. It soon appeared that nobody could go in a straight line, possibly due to the rear-wheel steering. So, progress was slow and, although not as exciting as expected, was highly amusing.

That was until the French Police arrived, and the farce really began. Turning up in a Police marked 2CV and wearing the flat hat and small cape associated with the incompetence in the Pink Panther movies could have been a better start. The fact that a bunch of drunken seafarers outran them up the gangway before they could get out of the car was another low point until it eventually got even worse.

The Gendarmerie started to shout to the Captain from the quayside in broken English. As childish as it was, it reminded us of the Pink Panther again. The more we laughed, the more irate they became. The Captain refused a request to come aboard, and the howls of derision emanating from that was making them irrationally angry. The crew shone deck lights at them until they pulled out guns and pointed them in our direction with a threat to shoot the lights out.

The joy and laughter on board were now uncontrollable. As these two clowns trooped up and down the quayside, frustrated and inept. Then the finale to finish off our night as they returned to their 2CV and it wouldn't start.

They finally left the stage, pushing their police car like some broken clown act as the party got into full swing on board.

Drunken English -1

French Gendarmes - Nil

GUNS & PIZZA

The two barrels of the shotgun were now pointing at my chest from a range of two feet. The finger appeared to be sweaty and trembling on the trigger. I didn't move.

The evening had started innocently in a bar, as most stories do. This one was in Biloxi, Mississippi, a small seaside holiday town northeast of New Orleans. A trip to the shopping mall had led to a few afternoon beers, a disco, and eventually meeting some local girls in the small hours of the morning. The English accent was again working its charms, and the girls asked us to join them for pizza at three in the morning. Finding a decent pizza in England in 1980 was hard enough finding one at 3 am was impossible. Here we had a choice of establishments to choose from, and we ended up in a Pizza Hut at 3 am.

The pizza was excellent, the company was pleasant, and all was very English, well-behaved and properly done until we left the restaurant. Two girls and three drunken Englishmen headed off into the night in a large green Ford until we sat at the traffic junction onto the main coast road through the town. It was probably 30 seconds at the red light, but it seemed like 30 minutes. No traffic anywhere and a red light for no reason, so our American girl driver jumped it and turned left onto the highway.

Within minutes blue lights behind were closing in on us, and we had been caught. As we went to pull over, we realised this was not what it seemed. Two police cars descended quickly, boxing us in front and back whilst another was across the road. I watched as the police car's doors flew open, and officers emerged with what looked like sawn-off shotguns. And when it was pointed at me with the order not to move, the adrenalin that kicked into my system was the fastest sobering process I have ever experienced. The real worry for me was that the officer holding the shotgun was also clearly nervous and appeared to be twitching his finger on the trigger. I was certainly not going to give him any reason to be more stressed than he already was.

We were led off one by one and leant against the police cars with our hands on the roof. It all appeared over the top for a red-light offence. However, the officers had calmed down considerably, having assessed that we were young, English, very drunk and highly unlikely to be carrying a gun. As I stood with my hands on the car's roof, the officers had a pow-wow in the middle of the closed road. With the window open, I could see the rack between the driver and passenger, which had held the sawn-off shotgun. As I reviewed the extensive police paraphernalia around the car with interest, the radio suddenly burst into life. The message was that the suspect had been apprehended in the car park of the Holiday inn.

"The people you want are at the Holiday inn", I shouted. "It's just been on your radio".

They left immediately with blue lights and sirens but without apology. However, they did have the decency to explain that the suspect had robbed Pizza Hut just after we left and was driving the same green Ford car. As we drove back to the ship with the adrenalin in my system subsiding, I remember going past the Holiday Inn car park. Through my returning drunken haze, I could see a green Ford like ours surrounded by dozens of police cars. But I was thinking, why so many cars for one man when they have shotguns anyway? One shotgun pointed at me was enough to get me to conform without argument.

And that was the end of the strangest episode and the scariest 10 seconds of my life.

We never did see the Biloxi girls again, but they certainly gave us a night we will never forget.

THE PERFECT CRIME

"Can you come with me, sir"? The armed officer said as he escorted me from the bar stool.

"What have I done, officer," I said in my best and most innocent English accent.

"Bring the bird, please, sir".

"Oh, the bird, but that's not mine. I was just given it at the bar". His grip on my arm tightened, and the sight of the gun in the holster persuaded me to comply. But, despite the sobering effect of being led off by an armed officer, I instinctively knew that my best English accent had slipped into more of a drunken slur. This was probably unidentifiable to sober people of any nationality yet strangely understood by drunks of all nationalities.

I found myself in a small office with two of my partners in crime sheepishly looking across the table at me. At the same time, another was led in. The bird was placed centrally on the table in front of us. The bird in question was a wire-framed plaster seagull with a 6ft wingspan that dominated the space in the room. It now had slightly less than 6ft of wingspan as a section was missing from one wing, and the wire poked out precariously towards me. I thought, wow, it didn't look that big hanging from the ceiling above the dancefloor. Then I realised I had said the statement aloud as the group around me started sniggering, and the manager looked stern and official. I noticed the police officers also trying to stifle a snigger, but maybe that was wishful thinking.

It was such a good idea when we thought of it. Where did it all go wrong? The plan was simple a seagull was flapping up and down over the dance floor that would look really good in the ship's bar. It only looks light, probably paper mâché, and we could reach it from the rails around the dance floor to cut the strings. One could catch it on the dance floor and pass it to me at the bar to hide between my legs. The reality was different. It was much bigger when it was off the ceiling, but 6 feet wide? We didn't expect that. We also didn't expect it to be made of very heavy and fragile plaster. Of course, we didn't expect to get caught either.

We had managed the cut, the catch, the pass and the hide. The hide was my task and, unfortunately, the least successful part of the plan. This was because a 6-foot-wide bird does not hide easily between your feet and a bar. In fact, it went across the feet of the two people on either side of me too. Add to that the trails of plaster from the broken wing and the number of people whacked across various parts of the body as it was "smuggled" very openly across a crowded bar and dance floor. But, of course, it would never be the crime of the century. Regardless of all those problems, we hadn't planned to get it out of the club anyway.

So here we were with a broken seagull, an armed guard and two police officers. There was a deal to be had, but we would be losers either way. The police clearly did not want the paperwork of reporting a damaged seagull, so compensation was the key, and a hasty negotiation process commenced. Negotiation was rather a grand description of the drunken garbled bargaining match. We were wasting our time because the bar owner obviously had a figure in mind that he would settle on. That figure was $200, so we were ripped off to the tune of $50 each to let us walk free, and that didn't even include keeping the seagull.

I recommend that if you want to take something from a bar, make sure it fits in your pocket first.

CHICAGO OR BUST

I can still see it," I said "I think we have driven around in a circle."

"It can't be a circle. We are on the edge of Lake Michigan. It's over 20,000 sq. miles, and we have only been driving for twenty minutes," was John's quick and entirely factual response.

The roads were getting narrower and more deserted, worryingly so, as we turned left and right repeatedly like a mouse in a laboratory maze. The neighbourhood was not one we wanted to be in. Industrial and run down, it had seen better days and better residents at some stage in its development. It was undoubtedly now on a downward spiral, and we appeared to be caught in that spiral, desperately looking for a route out and back to the safety and certainty of the interstate highway. At least a main road with traffic and public movement to let us know we were back in civilisation. It was the first time since being in America that I wanted to see a McDonald's.

The girls persevered in their driving, and although clearly a little concerned, they managed to keep calm and focused while the Englishmen in the back got seriously worried.

The girls diverted our attention by asking if the evening was worthwhile. It had been a long and challenging drive from Kenosha to Chicago and all to see a concert. Sixty-five miles didn't appear to be a long distance on the freeway, but we hadn't accounted for getting deep into the middle of the city. This was before mobile phones and google maps, so it was follow the signs and ask directions. Unfortunately, when looking for a theatre, there are so many in a city that misdirection is very common, as we found out to our cost on many occasions. We also made the schoolboy error of asking where the theatre was when what we really needed was somewhere to park near the theatre.

Chicago was just as it looked in the movies, immense, intense and downright confusing to drive in. Hence, after many directions to turn down one-way streets or arrive at the wrong theatre, we eventually found the one we wanted. To be more accurate, we found it three times as we kept driving past, unable to stop or find anywhere to park in the vicinity. Finally, by pure luck, a space became available on the street, and we arrogantly held up half of the Chicago traffic whilst we waited for the occupant to load everything in, check his seatbelt and mirrors twice, adjust his seat and eventually move out.

At last, we were two Englishmen with two American girls in the middle of Chicago on a midweek evening. It had been a last-minute decision just that afternoon to drive to Chicago when the four of us realised we were all Genesis fans. I was discussing seeing them at Knebworth six weeks before. More accurately, I was describing being unable to see them from the back of a field half a mile from the stage. That is when the girls said they were playing in Chicago that evening, and the plan was initiated immediately. There was only one flaw in the plan; to me, it was a massive one. We had no tickets. Admittedly we had a plan 'B', which was to make a tourist trip around Chicago, but now we were there, we wanted to see Genesis.

We walked to the theatre door, already downhearted. It was clear from the noise leaking out from the theatre that the show had already started, and the box office was shut. However, a few dodgy-looking characters were checking us out as we approached. They were ticket touts, and although fearing the worst and expecting failure, we approached anyway. "Do you need tickets?" they asked," I have four available, good seats".

"But the show has already started", I replied dejectedly. The tout seemed a little taken back, partly by my lack of interest and also by my accent. His attitude softened immediately, and he asked the obvious American question.

"Are you English?" followed by the inevitable "I love your accent". Anyone travelling in America will be familiar with the comment and conversations that follow. There is usually some distant English relative involved or a friend in London, and do we know them? Undoubtedly, it was an icebreaker, and the Touts had gathered around and were keenly conversing with us about why and how we were there. Without asking or making any offers for tickets, we suddenly had four thrust towards us. "Sixty dollars he said.

"We can't afford that type of money. The concert's already started anyway," I replied.

"Sixty is cheap", he responded," look, these are Twenty Dollar tickets".

"Yes, and you want three times the price," I said indignantly.

"No", he responded with what looked like a genuine affront to his character ", it's sixty for all four of them". I must have stepped back in shock before eagerly reaching out to take the tickets and examine them. They did look genuine, and they were printed at $20 each. We were right next to the door of the theatre, so if they were fakes, we would find out immediately. With little to lose and everything to gain, I handed him Sixty dollars, and we walked into the theatre.

As we walked in at the back of the stalls, the noise hit us like a wave, but what struck us next was the small scale of the theatre. After the vast expanse of Knebworth, this was a regular theatre of approximately 2,500 seats with the band in clear view right in front of us. Ushers still existed in those days, and as we were led down the aisle, we could not believe our luck as we got closer and closer to the stage. Our row was about 16 from the stage, but it felt like we were on the stage with them.

Two hours later, with our ears still ringing from the noise, we sat in a small American car on a backstreet of Chicago, reminiscing and hoping we were not about to get carjacked or shot. Then, finally, after what seemed like a lifetime but was probably about fifteen minutes, we could see a highway alongside the road we were on. We stayed with it on and off for some miles, sometimes closer and sometimes further away, until we eventually came to a junction that connected. I wouldn't say it was a slip-road or even authorised access. It was more like an old maintenance access for police and repair vehicles: no signs and no merging lane, just a straight entrance onto the carriageway. We didn't care, to us it was sanctuary, and even if we got arrested for using it, we would have been happy to be in police custody.

So, I had seen Genesis twice in six weeks and much more of Chicago than I wanted to. Unfortunately, after the stress of the evening, we saw a lot less of our American chauffeurs than we wanted to, but we will be forever grateful for their driving and survival techniques.

P is for Pis...a

"He is not dead. He has not had a heart attack." We were shouting simultaneously now, all three of us, as they once again tried to load the stretcher, complete with Alan on board, into the ambulance.

The ambulance crew gesticulated wildly in that stereotypical Mediterranean way. They were shouting in Italian, which none of us understood. We did understand the hand gestures of hand hitting the chest to say he has had a heart attack. They pulled the stretcher into the ambulance as we pulled it back out. It became a mad Chuckle brothers sketch, to me, to you, to me, to you. All this was being played out in a beautiful square in Livorno in front of a captivated Italian public who earnestly went about their evening business. This mainly consisted of eating, drinking and calling ambulances to deal with drunken Scotsmen lying prostrate on the grass. The fact that the three of us had not even noticed he was missing until the blue lights turned up was worrying. It was also a testament to the quantity of cheap Italian wine consumed that day.

What else are you to do when you finish the day's work on the ship docked in Livorno? Decide to catch some culture by seeing the Leaning Tower of Pisa instead of going to the pub? Thus, radio officer Dan and engineers Alan and Dave joined me in our search for culture. This should be applauded, especially when we realised it was a one and a half hour's bus ride to Pisa. Sitting on a crowded bus for hours, we were desperate for toilets, entertainment and a drink when we got to Pisa. That was before we realised that we also had another mile and a half to walk after we got off the bus. No mobile phones and google maps in those days either. That meant directions from Italians in broken English, which equates to a two-and-a-half mile walk once all the detours are taken.

But we persisted in our culture search and arrived at the tower just before 8 pm. The evening was bright, so photos were taken, and most of them were ultimately left in the camera on a bus in Rotterdam, but that is another story. We were impressed, and it was worth the journey. Our engineering brains were astounded at the angle it was leaning and how it was still standing. After such a journey and loss of drinking time, we eagerly approached the gate to buy a ticket and go to the top of this marvellous structure.

"Mi dispiace, siamo chuisi," said the chap in an official-looking uniform at the gate. Italians like a uniform, and all look very authoritative no matter their role. This chap was obviously the Pisa bouncer deciding whom to let in and whom to evict for wearing the wrong trainers. A family entered a few minutes before us as we approached the gate. " Mi dispiace, siamo chuisi," he said once again. We reached into our pockets and offered a handful of Lira only to have it refused. " Mi dispiace, siamo chuisi," he repeated as he started waving his hands in a cross-motion and pointing to the sign behind him.

It dawned on us suddenly that he was saying the tower was closed. It was just past eight o clock, and we tried to explain to him in charades the long and challenging trip we had undertaken from England to get here just to climb this tower. I believe we got the message across, but he wasn't for moving even when offered financial bribery in keeping with the traditional Italian business model. The rope in front of us was easily skipped over or around. Still, the power of the uniform was too strong, and we walked away, shoulders slumped, beaten, bruised and thirsty.

And so, the evening started. A local bar, a bottle of wine each and an hour to fill waiting for a bus back to Livorno. We had another bottle each to liven up the bus journey back. Arriving in Livorno, we alighted from the bus in a beautiful square with a park in the centre, surrounded by shops, small bars and a cinema. So, we continued the evening with a few more beers, moving from bar to bar around the square until the blue lights arrived. At that stage, we realised that our wee Scotsman Alan had not followed us from the last bar but had laid down on the grass in the middle of the square.

Thus, the pantomime started until the truth finally dawned on the ambulance crew. They suddenly tipped Alan off the stretcher onto the grass in true chuckle Brothers style. Then, they slammed their doors before roaring off into the sunset, shouting what we could only assume to be Italian obscenities.

What can you do after that except have another beer? It was clear from Alan's disposition, slumped half unconscious over the rail, being sick onto the grass, that we needed to take him back to the ship. It was fortunate but probably not surprising that big Dave, built like a six-foot-two rugby player, was the most sober. Alan, meanwhile, was five foot five and easy to carry. It was not so fortunate that the taxi rank was in the square, and they had all witnessed the events of the last twenty minutes.

The line of taxis was impressive, but their customer service was not. Each one refused to take us for fear of Alan re-decorating their lovely clean interiors. Lengthy discussions took place, and eventually, an agreement was reached with one entrepreneur who saw an opportunity to cash in by charging the cleaning fee before any cleaning was necessary. This was four times the going rate on the meter. The deal was struck, and we took the most expensive taxi ride in Europe back to the ship.

The next day Alan remembered nothing about his escapades, and like a true Scotsman, he believes we made the whole thing up to get back at him for the excess taxi fare.

DON'T GO INTO THE LIGHT

"Come on, you pisshead, it's 8.20, ". I shouted to Neil, still under his bed covers.

"The second (engineer) will be wondering where you are soon. Get your arse out of bed and in the engine room". The response was a brief grunt which was an improvement on the previous one, so progress was being made. I had been on the overnight generator watch while the rest of the engineers had been ashore in Hamburg and obviously partaken heavily of the local brew. It was often me in the position that Neil found himself now, but although I could empathise, I was in no mood to compromise after a fourteen hour shift. I was tired and hungry and hadn't even had the pleasure of a night in Hamburg.

In an attempt to wake him, I started asking open questions about this evening.

"Did you have a good night? Where did you go? What did you get up to?" I was rewarded with another grunt and, eventually, a movement. He rolled over slowly, and in answer to all three questions, an arm protruded from the blankets and gestured across the room. Following the trajectory and in the near total darkness of the room, my eyes started to focus on a large dark object in the corner.

As I approached and my eyes got more accustomed to the gloom. I noticed that this was a very large object that eventually came into focus as a pile covered by a large grey blanket. I would say my thoughts were racing, but with the tiredness in my brain, it was best described as slowly crawling to a conclusion on what may be under this grey mass. My first thought was that I hoped it wasn't a stray person or animal picked up on a drunken walk back to the ship. My second thought was if it was a person or animal, I hoped it was alive and ok or had the evening gone way over the top disastrously? There were no other thoughts because my brain could function no further than that, so I grabbed the blanket and pulled it off swiftly.

The shock of what confronted me made me jump back, and as I stumbled onto Neil's shoes underfoot, I fell backwards, ending up on my backside. Suddenly my senses were overcome by going from almost total darkness straight into the path of a jumbo Jet with all lights aimed at me. The room was suddenly like a scene from Saturday Night Fever. Not just brightly lit in a blindingly bright orange glow, it was also strobing in a mixed haphazard fashion that simultaneously disorientated and confused. My first thought was to turn it off, and I scrambled across the floor for the blanket, which I threw back over the pile. This action covered about three-quarters of the pile, leaving me the chance to assess the situation in a now illuminated but more subdued environment.

The explanation was now glaringly obvious. At least a dozen bright orange road works warning lights lay before me. All turned on and all flashing with a different sequence to produce an overpowering intensity and frequency of bright orange light.

Before I could ask Neil the next obvious question, I felt a movement behind me. The brightness of this collection had woken the undead. Neil was up and groaning, shuffling around like a mummy from a bad horror movie. "For god's sake, cover them up again. They kept me awake half the night". He groaned.

"Where did you get them?" I asked. As soon as I asked it, I realised it was a stupid question. I corrected it instantly. "Did you take these from a road works?" Another stupid question, but it had to be asked to lead to the next one.

"It wasn't just me", Neil responded.

"I realise that", I said, "you can't carry this many alone. I have thoughts of a pile of cars in the bottom of a hole somewhere in Hamburg."

"It's ok. There were cones as well, and we left them there."

"Why didn't you turn off the lights?"

"We didn't know how."

I picked up one of the bright orange lights, now flashing manically in my hand. Unfortunately, there didn't appear to be a switch. The battery compartment was screwed up, so I could not remove them easily. Then I spotted a small hole in the side. "Have you got a match?" I asked, knowing Neil was a terrible chain smoker. He produced a box from beside his bed, and I took a match and gently probed into the hole at the side of the lamp. It went off. Neil and I cheered simultaneously and sighed, relieved that the crisis was over.

A year and several different ships later, I re-joined the same ship, the Magdalena. As I walked into the bar, I couldn't help laughing out loud. There in front of me, around the top of the bar itself, was a line of bright orange road lights. A permanent fixture of the ship for all who sailed on her. But a personal memory for just Neil and myself.

ST JOHNS SURPRISE

"I can't serve you, you are banned." "But I have never been here before. This is a new bar to me, and this is my first time in New Brunswick," I replied to the girl behind the bar.

"You are banned from last night", she replied

This was a confusing situation made all the worse because, in 1982, there was no internet, Facebook, Twitter, digital cameras or any way of getting information around quickly and easily. So what had I gotten up to last night that resulted in this cruel and unjust punishment? It was made even worse by my hangover. It was midday, and we had ventured out of the engine room to seek a dinner-time beer to ease the pain and aid recovery.

We were in a small bar near the dock area, as far removed from town and the clubs of last night as you could get. Yet I was banned. How could this be? Andy was with me and was allowed a beer, so he ordered, and we started the investigation with the barmaid.

How was I banned from drinking in the whole of St. Johns, New Brunswick, after just one night in town?

I remembered the unfortunate popcorn incident that occurred in our first bar early in the afternoon. That could not be considered a drinking incident as it was our first drink, and we were sober, although we did not hang around long enough to prove that to the manager at the time.

Sitting at the end of the hotel bar, I watched in interest as the barmaid filled and turned on a large popcorn machine. This was now popping its hot and tasty contents into an empty sink next to it for the barmaid to scoop out full bowls of popcorn for the tables. Fascinated by this and not keen to wait for our bowl to arrive, I reached across and tried a handful directly from the machine. At that moment, I learnt how hot fresh popcorn can be. Whilst not burning hot, the shock was enough for me to pull my hand away quickly and knock the discharge spout of the machine, which started to wobble, then as if in slow motion, it toppled backwards while continuing to discharge popcorn. The result was a broadside of hot popcorn being fired across the bar at several tables of unsuspecting drinkers who looked very surprised at the new express delivery service. As quick as the delivery service was, it was not as quick as our exit out of the door behind us. Surely that couldn't have got me banned?

Further investigation revealed that the barmaid worked in the only nightclub in town, and she had witnessed my eviction from it the previous evening. So, the reality was that I was only banned where she worked. Unfortunately, that appeared to be the few places I wanted to drink in, as St Johns was not a huge town.

I felt it was all an injustice, and I was being blamed for the crimes of others. So yes, I was thrown out of the club, but I was with

Dave, the Fourth Engineer, and our reasons for eviction were very different.

I was weary after a long day of eating too much popcorn and maybe a few beers. I could have left, but I felt the need to stay and support Dave while he tried his best to chat up a lovely young girl at the bar. Unfortunately, while the barman warned me not to sleep at the bar, he noticed Dave chatting up his girlfriend. Unfortunately for Dave, he was a tall, handsome chap the girls loved but bouncers didn't particularly like. And that is how we both ended up head first in a six foot snowdrift after being thrown head first in a truly comical Hollywood manner. A sobering experience, you may think, but the sobriety didn't last long, and I remember the torturously slow walk back to the ship downhill on frozen pavements with no coordination like Bambi on ice.

So, there I was in St Johns, a small town with few bars, and I couldn't get a drink. It's a good job we were sailing the same day and even better that no modern media existed so that it was forgotten in time to return and party again six weeks later.

No popcorn next time.

HOLY F**K

Holy fuck was not a statement I expected to hear from Harry. I certainly didn't think he would shout it out for the whole ship to hear.

Harry was our ship's electrician and a committed and practising Sikh, very polite and always well-spoken. Yet on this occasion, I think his god could forgive him due to mitigating circumstances. It was August 1984 and we were on the M.V. Barrydale sailing under a Panamanian flag. The day before, we had docked in Beirut Lebanon, having been diverted there just three days earlier. Despite appearing to be at war for several years, Beirut was officially classified as a conflict zone and the world service had confirmed a cease-fire across the city.

So here we were, preparing to unload bananas with one of the ship's cranes out of action. I was sailing as Second Engineer and had good knowledge and confidence in most aspects of the Barrydale in its previous life as the Magdalena. My weak point was the unpredictable and unreliable Electro Hydraulic cranes. I had assisted in repairing them on many occasions but in all honesty, it was more luck than good judgement that got them operational each time. I don't think I was alone in this confusion. They always appeared to be more of a dark art than a logical approach. Thankfully Harry was assisting me this time and he was a very capable electrician.

Having twiddled with some valves and hit things with hammers, the crane was functioning again and we were leaving the cab via the short vertical ladder. As we did so, our backs were to the quayside and the city itself. we could not see behind us, but we could hear and what we heard was the loud whistle of an approaching shell. We stopped still on the ladder, wary of moving in any direction. The sound was clearly coming in our direction and getting closer. Adjacent to us on the next quay was a shipwreck sitting on the harbour floor with just the bridge deck above the water. The bridge had a shell hole dead centre. Was that to be our fate? We clung tighter to the ladder as if it could offer us any protection and said nothing as the sound reached a peak. Was this it, was it going to drop now? Thankfully not. The sound started to diminish as we heard the shell go over the top of our heads and towards the open sea. It hit the water with a splash but no explosion. Simultaneously, Harry released his emotions with the loudest "Holly Fuck" I have ever heard.

We scrambled down the last rungs of the ladder and I immediately sought a beer to calm my nerves. Meanwhile, teetotaller Harry went off to pray for forgiveness, muttering under his breath about the need for a crash turban.

Although we were paid three times our normal pay rate for the days spent in Beirut, it still felt very uncomfortable and we were keen to get away as soon as possible. Apart from the two shipwrecks in the harbour, there were young teenagers walking around with machine guns firing randomly into the water and a nightly display of firepower from each side of the city. This happened at 7 pm each evening and consisted of the north and south sides of the city firing shells at a tower block in the central area. The block itself was so full of holes there didn't seem much left to hit but they still fired at it for 30 minutes every night. To my surprise, each side had a different colour tracer which created a spectacular nightly light show for all on board.

The risk was such that we were not allowed off the ship and there was an armed guard at the gangway to prevent undesirables from coming on board. The real danger of the situation was highlighted when the buyer of the cargo arrived at the ship. He had more security than an American president and arrived in a convoy of six black limousines filled with armed guards.

It was strange that in this war-torn environment where bananas were scarce enough to become a valuable commodity, there was a thriving black market in watches and digital technology. The only time we were allowed onto the quayside was one afternoon when a group of salesmen turned up with suitcases full of the latest electronics. Watches were always a popular purchase for seafarers as they were usually much cheaper abroad than in the UK. Seiko was the most popular make but the latest battery analogue and LCD digital ones were now more accurate and affordable. Here in this worn torn city, they had all the latest big brands and more at bargain prices.

It was an opportunity to buy desirable and useful presents instead of the usual tacky tourist items. There were a few places on my trips where good gifts could be found, including rugs and leather from Egypt and my personal favourite, a carved shark from Pitcairn Island in the Pacific. With a population of 45 on 18 square miles, the descendants of the Mutiny on the Bounty received their Royal Mail via passing Shaw Savill ships. I was lucky enough to stop there en-route to New Zealand and help out their tiny economy by buying a hand-carved shark, which is the only souvenir I retain to this day. Unique and signed on the back by its maker and kept for the memory it evokes rather than its artistic quality.

TURBO CURRY

As we stepped off the gangway into the dugout canoe, it felt that we had just stepped back into a simpler time.

It was a time when boats were actually dug out of tree trunks by large skilled men with axes in jungle clearings. It was surprisingly broad and accommodating for a dugout canoe. This was a huge tree trunk, and as the four of us sat down with the boatman, it felt surprisingly stable and comfortable. We were now looking up at the side of the ship. The Matina was a 7,000-tonne refrigerated ship, basically a vast floating fridge designed to carry bananas. The side next to us was sheer and vertical for 60 feet or more of bright white metal that totally dominated our small canoe, yet to the right of us was a view of the Columbian jungle.

There was no jetty here in Turbo, unlike all other banana ports. The banana plantations were in the jungle clearings, and the town was on the edge of the massive bay we were now anchored in. Bananas were loaded onto huge barges and floated out to the ship to be loaded with the ship's derricks. Barges full of workers also came out with bananas each day. A small floating town of activity would set up around the ship bringing life, music and vitality until the end of the working day when they floated back home again.

I had been to Turbo many times but had yet to go ashore to see the town. This was an opportunity I could not miss. The juxtaposition between the ship and the jungle could not have been more intense. Sitting in a real dugout canoe, I felt I was about to cross a boundary from first-world to third in an instant.

That thought was instantly shattered by the sound of a huge Yamaha outboard motor roaring into life. The outboard was on the back of the canoe, immediately bringing the ancient and modern world in direct contact, utilising old and new technologies and creating a blurring of the precise boundaries that no longer exist anywhere in the world. Western civilisation, as we arrogantly call it, has invaded all areas of the world and often negatively impacted societies better formed and balanced than ours. This was the case in Columbia, where the West's desire for illegal drugs had fuelled their growth and trade in the land in which they grew so well. Cash crops had pushed food crops out of the fields, and organised criminal gangs now managed and dictated to farmers.

Even in Turbo, where the whole economy was based on bananas, an underlying feeling of aggression was in the air, fuelled by gangs of youths with little to do in an isolated one-horse town where poverty was the usual way of life. The company owned the plantations, the railway that took the bananas to the town and the town itself. In effect, they owned the people who were cheap and flexible workers who had no choice. It is obvious in this one-sided relationship that the promise of easy money would attract young men into the comparative cash affluent world of cocaine.

The town itself was little more than a shanty town but with a strange mix of real buildings with purpose and structure and many little more than shacks that a strong wind could remove. The road around the town was more like a series of interconnected potholes. This was irrelevant as there was no road into town to get a vehicle in or out. Despite this, the status symbol was a car, and there were six that we saw during our brief visit. Each was parked outside a house with a group of youths sitting in, on or around it. They were always playing music and sometimes revving the engine with nowhere to go. Occasionally one would venture onto the 'road' and begin the precarious circular route around town, dipping into and out of potholes violently as they went. The occupants were often on the roof or bonnet. They would hold on for their life. They were grinning at the knowledge that those watching linked their presence with the owner of a car. The perfect example of the Columbian style of success by association.

All too quickly, we realised that we had seen all that Turbo had to offer. So, we gravitated to the alternative reason for the precarious canoe trip, which was to have a Chinese meal. Yes, in this desolate one-horse, six-car town, there was a Chinese restaurant regularly frequented by the ship's crew seeking a change from the regular fare on board. Food on the ship was ok, but after several months, a change is always welcome.

The restaurant was surprisingly large, with a dozen tables or more, about a third occupied at the time. I don't know what we expected. But we didn't expect the ornate red and gold decorations with banners, dragons and lions that we were familiar with in Chinese restaurants back home. Here we were on the edge of a jungle in the familiar surroundings of a Chinese Restaurant that could be anywhere in the world. But we weren't anywhere in the world. We were physically on the edge of a jungle, sitting with it just ten feet from our table. We did not need to see the jungle, we just had to listen.

The noises were like a David Attenborough documentary with numerous animals, birds and insects vying for attention in a cacophony of noise. We ordered chicken curry and had a rum and coke while we waited. Whilst not a spirit drinker by choice, this was always the safest bet in Central America. The beers did not always travel well, and getting cold ones was difficult, but the rum and the coke were often made locally and were cost-effective and strong. We had carried coke concentrate in barrels to many of these ports, where they were reconstituted in small local factories. The only other drink available everywhere we went was Guinness, but only in bottles, of which I was never a fan.

Our curry came and was a welcome change to the ship's menu. Whilst very tasty, we noticed that the chicken bones were tiny, definitely white meat and tasty but small. Only when we had finished did someone reflect on the major population in the adjacent jungle, and we all took time out to concentrate and look closer.

The greenery was intense, particularly in the high canopy of the trees. Still, as we focused, we saw that not all the green was the tree canopy itself. Hundreds and hundreds of green parakeets filled the bright green canopy and made much of the noise. These were beautiful birds, and they exposed yellow plumage under their wings when they flew. But, sitting in the trees, they were almost invisible within the canopy. The hundreds we could see were within the trees closest to us, but there were trees as far as the eye could see, all populated with the same intensity.

It dawned on us that the local food resource was probably parakeets and that we had just eaten a parakeet curry. This in itself was not alarming. It is just another bird, but what amused us was that our $5 curry probably contained £800 of ingredients if bought in a UK pet shop. So, it remains to this day, quite possibly my best value meal ever.

FOOLS AND HORSES

"Excuse me sirs, would you mind moving into the lounge area while I vacuum the lawn."

Astroturf may be a common sight nowadays, but in 1983, the sight of a man vacuuming a hotel lawn was not the usual start to my day. It was apparent that unusual was becoming the new normal in my life. Here I was with Andy Thompson sitting in a posh hotel in Valparaiso, Chile drinking a beer at 11 am while a man was vacuuming the lawn. Around us, the guests seemed relaxed, outside the sun shone, and everything was normal. In fact, it was positively buzzing. As a holiday destination for the Capital, Santiago, just 60 miles away, Valparaiso was desirable for those Chileans who could afford it.

We were not on holiday and didn't want to be there at all, but having paid off our ship after six months at sea, we now had a four-day wait for the next flight to the UK. So, we were determined to make the most of it. The night before, we had visited the local area, including a lovely seaside walk and even a rather fancy casino that looked out of our financial league. Hence, we were happy with the excuse that we were not dressed for it. Knowing the history of Chile's famous coup less than ten years ago, we were surprised to see this affluence with fancy cars and well-dressed people with money to gamble. Still, we said ten years is a long time in politics.

However, as we ventured closer to the town centre, we were to discover that this was a country of opposites and conflicts. Getting away from the tourist area, we were greeted by warm and welcoming bars and even warmer and welcoming people. One particular bar sticks in the memory for several reasons but mainly for the real-life realisation of the oldest joke in the book.

The bar was long and thin, running between two streets with entrances at each end. The bar ran the entire length allowing people to sit and lean along its generous proportions, whilst tables ran along the opposite wall. Basically, it was a long corridor selling beer. The nature of it created a unique atmosphere, with the two entrances creating a pass-through with a chat and beer on the way. We discovered this design feature's additional advantage and popularity later that night. The bar staff here, as everywhere, were friendly and chatty. Interested in talking to someone with an English accent, the subjects always included football and their political situation and recent history. But this was always discussed in hushed tones as though some unseen authority was still judging opinions. There was a disquiet when the subject was raised. And nervousness in those around us, even if they were not involved in the conversation.

During one such earnest and hushed conversation, the mood was lightened for

Andy and me by an event totally disregarded by those around. They could not understand why we were in fits of laughter for a prolonged and repeated period. Neither could they understand our constant requests for the barman to do it again.

We were sitting at the bar with a view above half of the bar and the optics behind. When the barman walked along from the left behind the bar, as he got to our position, he seemed to get suddenly shorter, then continued to do so with each step. It was the classic pretend-to-walk downstairs gag. But the trick was that he didn't come back up. He really had walked down the cellar steps, which he had opened discreetly behind the bar using a pulley. It was a perfectly executed move right in front of us, and we applauded and cheered as he reappeared up the steps back into the room. David Blaine couldn't have done it better. It was that only fools and horses' moment, and our night was complete whatever else happened.

Little were we to know what was going to happen. We started our bar tour early in the afternoon. As time moved on, it was still early, before 9 pm, when the bar clientele started to thin out considerably. It was then that the barman approached and informed us of a night-time curfew. The hotel had mentioned this, but in a country listed as politically stable and in a holiday resort, it was surprising that it was so clearly observed and worried about by local people. We were fine as outsiders. We were free to move around, but almost certainly, we would be challenged on the street at some stage in the evening. This happened twice on our way back to the hotel, and we had a pleasant chat with two gentlemen with submachine guns on each occasion.

With this knowledge, we reviewed our evening in the bar. Particularly the movement of people through the bar from one street to the other. It became apparent that the number of curfew monitors on the street was limited. The bar was the ideal cut-through that allowed avoidance by choosing the right exit at the right time.

It was the perfect bar in the ideal location for the political climate of the time, with Del Boy thrown in for good measure.

THE GODFATHER

I gave my customary wave towards the gatehouse window as George and I entered the dock gate.

It was later than we had planned to be walking back to the ship, and we certainly hadn't expected such late drinking in the local pubs. Nevertheless, here we were, entering the dock gates of Sheerness in the early hours of the morning. It was our third day in Sheerness docks, so we knew the way around and had no safety worries. We still regretted our delayed walk because the first raindrops started to fall as we entered the gates.

We were now regretting the decision not to take coats into town earlier that evening. The rain became heavy very quickly and being late October, the low night temperature and wet clothes were not a good mix. It was still three-quarters of a mile from the entrance to the ship's berth. I knew that as we ventured into the site, we needed to take a left fork to get to the ship. I also knew that this was a long and diverse route that diverted around many storage areas containing the tractors that we would load and take to Wisconsin. George and I discussed the potential for a shorter route if we took the right fork and decided to split the difference. I went right. He went left. The best man wins.

Fifteen minutes later, I walked around the end of a warehouse with the sea in full view. Disappointingly, although I was on the quay, it was the wrong quay. I could see the ship, but it was on an adjacent quay separated by a 20-foot gap. Wet, cold and frustrated, I cursed my stupidity and returned the way I came. Halfway back towards the left fork, I found and took a different left turn. Confident that was the real shortcut, I proceeded with new enthusiasm.

Once again, I could see the sea and quayside as I turned around the final corner of a warehouse. Devastatingly I was back on the same quay that was still the wrong one.

Extremely cold and tired now, the alcohol in my system started to play tricks with my mind. I looked at the gap between the two quays. The 20-foot gap now looked smaller than earlier. Not small enough to jump but possibly small enough to swim, I thought. Fortunately, common sense still existed at the back of my alcohol fuelled brain cells. My common sense pointed out that there was a 15-foot drop to the water with no way to get out at the other side. The water would be freezing cold and a real shock to the system. Then there were the simple practicalities of being fully clothed. No such issues as mobile phones in 1978, but what would I do with my wallet and watch? Fortunately, I made the smart choice to walk all the way back again, and this time I went the right way.

This was not always the case; one particular location springs to mind where several crew colleagues made the wrong choice. The location was Golfito, a small banana port in Costa Rica. Golfito was in a beautiful bay surrounded by jungle foliage and little patches of isolated golden beaches that could only be reached by boat. On the top of the hill overlooking the town was the Picnic Bar. There was a road to this bar set deep into the bush but also a shorter footpath. This was very steep, and anyone making the trek deserved extensive refreshment at the top whilst overlooking a beautiful tropical bay. From this high vantage point, the banana-loading jetty could clearly be seen to connect in one corner of the bay but then run parallel to the road along the front of the town. This road had most of the bars on it, so the ship was visible just 50 yards away at all times.

Whilst the jetty was in deep water, the vast patch of water separating it from the road was visibly shallow, with about 20 yards of the paddle-depth beach until it was deep enough to require swimming. Thus, in the mind of a drunken seafarer, all the negatives that stopped me in Sheerness were not there in Golfito. It was a shallow walk into the water. The water and air temperatures were warm, and they wore shorts and T-shirts with no wallets or watches. It is, therefore, no surprise how many have tried the swim, including several of my close friends. Fortunately, they turned back when in difficulty, and no one lost their lives. The message is that alcohol and swimming are a deadly mix wherever you are in the world.

Back in the harsh reality of a wet, cold English October night, I was elated as I eventually arrived at the bottom of the ship's gangway. The rain was now torrential as I started up the steps. Suddenly halfway up, I slipped, catching my right shin on the metal edge of a step. I stopped momentarily cursing with the pain. No matter how much alcohol you have in your system, hitting your shins is always a seriously painful experience. Unfortunately, I couldn't check the injury with my wet jeans stuck to my leg, so I continued up the gangway and hobbled off to my cabin.

The next thing I remember was being woken by the 4th engineer in the morning. I remember him telling me I needed to be up immediately or I would be late. As he spoke, he pulled the bed covers off to make sure I would get up. That's when I heard the scream and the statement.

"Fuck in hell, Dave, are you ok? Where's the horse's head?"

I sat up, immediately wondering what he meant, when I was shocked to see most of my bed sheets covered in blood. As I sat on the side of the bed, I recalled the fall on the gangway and looked down at my right leg. It was covered in dry blood, but so was most of me. There was no fresh bleeding, and as I gingerly washed around the wound, it turned out to be a simple but very bloody cut that had created a flap of skin. Obviously, every time I moved in bed, I was disturbing the flap and causing new bleeding. So, what appeared to be a major trauma required simple careful washing, a few days of dressing and a new set of bedsheets.

I still have the scar 45 years later, but no horse's head.

CAN I HAVE A VODKA WITH THAT?

"Twoje zdrowie", was the shout from across the table." Cheers", we replied as we raised the glasses to our lips and threw the hot, burning fire water down our throats. This was vodka, but not as we knew it.

We all reached for the small shot glasses of coke and threw them down to follow the vodka, hoping that it would cool the effect and we would not pull painful facial expressions that may upset our hosts. And what wonderful hosts they were. Here we were in Gdansk, Poland, when it was still behind the Iron Curtain of Russia. But, unknown to us, their world was about to change forever. The revolution was to take place right here in this very dockyard where we were unloading bananas. Maybe I even bumped into the future President of Poland,

Lech Walesa, as he worked in the shipyard as an electrician. Who knows?

I know we had landed in a country full of proud people oppressed to the point that it felt like a corked drink ready to pop. The Polish people were impressive, smart and friendly but also devious and cunning. That must come from building up survival techniques to live and develop in a society that restricts living and individuals' development for the state's sake. Yes, we were ripped off, changing our American dollars illegally in the street, but that comes with the territory. That's part of our learning curve and their survival. We were never in danger or felt threatened and always felt welcome. They had little but offered it to us if they could. Hence, we were now sitting in a private wedding. Three Englishmen side by side at a long table of Polish revellers and family to celebrate the wedding of a delightful young couple at the head of the table. We had a bottle of vodka each but had to pass around the coke and fill a little shot glass each time. Such was the nature of the politically driven economy of Poland.

It was the end of a long night and an even longer taxi journey. We had yet to realise how big Gdansk was. It was a large and impressive city. It should have been even more impressive, but it was all grey. It looked and felt grey as if we were in a permanent fog. It wasn't an actual fog, of course. It was the fog of oppression. The fact that the snow was two feet deep did help create a feeling of being in a black-and-white movie. Snow can often make the world seem brighter, but it was not working here in Gdansk.

The taxi ride from the port to town had been long, and we were worried about the cost, but it soon became apparent that we had more than enough money to last the night. We felt like we were being fleeced at every turn, and we probably were, but it was still cheap to us, and it looked like the locals could do with the extra cash, which was unlikely to be spent on drugs or flash cars. They didn't need it for vodka, which appeared everywhere and was as common and cheap as water. As long as you didn't want a mixer with it, that's when it got expensive.

We were not exotic or demanding. We simply wanted the basics in life, which at this time in the evening, was a beer. This simple request was often met with raised eyebrows and a shrug of the shoulders. This was followed by a long walk into a back room before three bottles appeared and were passed to us with a glass that was never big enough to hold the contents in one go. This came to a head when we were directed to a bar and restaurant in the centre of Gdansk. Like several others we had been to that afternoon, we felt like intruders. Not unwelcome but more like the stranger walking into the saloon in a western movie. This one was a small open doorway off the street. As we walked in, it instantly went up a steep flight of narrow stairs. This felt uncomfortable already, almost domestic in scale and decoration. It felt like we were about to emerge into someone's living room.

"Look on the bright side", I said. They may have a beer in the fridge. As we emerged at the top of the stairs, I was relieved to see it open out immediately into a large room. Directly in front of us was a bar, but no bar stools or standing area. To our right and stretching back behind us was a room full of tables sporadically populated by diners and drinkers. The décor was basic, with no soft furnishing or carpet to dampen the space. It felt a little like a school hall at dinner time. Looking for direction or instruction, we got a nod from the waitress standing at the bar with a tray in her hand. The nod was towards the empty table to the far side of the room. We made our way in that direction.

As we removed our coats to sit down, she stood waiting, pad in hand and pencil, ready to take our order. "Sorry, we don't speak Polish," we said, "we are English".

Her dour demeanour disappeared, and she smiled. "I English a little," she said proudly as she pulled a menu from her apron and thrust it in my direction.

"Just beer, please," I said. Then, in the traditional Englishman abroad manner, I felt the need to repeat it louder and slower in pigeon English. "Three", I held up three fingers for effect ", beers please", and I mimed the act of swigging a bottle. Of course, this could mean I wanted a drink of anything, so I could have ordered a bottle of vodka each. But, of course, we hadn't, and we had learnt enough from our travels around the world that beer is similar in every language except Spanish. We were just about to find out that it's also different in Polish, although it worked perfectly well all afternoon.

"Piwo," the waitress said back to us. Yes, that sounded close enough to beer, we thought and nodded in agreement as if we were suddenly fluent Polish speakers.

We sat and surveyed the room as we waited in anticipation for the waitress to return. The small round tables were mostly occupied by couples, except for an elderly man reading a large newspaper with regular sideways glances in our direction. It was reminiscent of a 1960s spy movie with us playing the part of the foreign spies. However, we were not doing a good job of it. Every eye in the room appeared to be focused on us at the time. Finally, we breathed a sigh of relief as the waitress appeared with a tray. The first reason was that she delivered three bottles of beer, not vodka. The second was that all eyes suddenly turned away in unison as if the choice of beer as a beverage flagged us as no longer of interest.

The beer was cold and tasted good. We considered the menu, but having looked around at the food served at the other tables, we decided to stick to a liquid diet for the evening. The beers were quickly consumed, and we were again seeking the waitress's attention. I held up three fingers, mouthing my new word Piwo as she approached the table.

She acknowledged this with a strange shake of the head. I feared my Polish accent had not been interpreted correctly, and at best, I had confused her or, at worst, insulted her. Fortunately, neither was the case as she started to explain in a mix of minimal broken English and Polish that we could not have a beer. The discussion, if it could be described as such, was long and very confusing. We wanted to know why, and she wanted to know what we wanted to drink instead. This led to a strange and confused listing of every possible alcoholic concoction she could provide, but we didn't want. Before we realised that, we were talking at cross purposes, two different conversations, in different languages, with no outcome whatsoever. We eventually stopped talking and smiled at each other. The word beer and a shrug of the shoulders was a much more helpful international language, and it worked here.

The waitress pointed to her wrist and the clock on the wall. With the use of fingers and a few more body signs later, we were now aware of why we could not have a beer. It was now after seven pm. Yes, unbelievably, they only served beer until 7 pm. After that, we could have anything but not beer. Finally, in desperation and thanks to the waitress, we ordered three vodkas and cokes that we didn't really want, and she went off with the smile of a job well done.

Three large vodkas duly appeared with a tiny bottle of coke between them. We drank them as we discussed our next move, which was about finding another beer. As we left, we approached the counter to leave a large tip for our helpful waitress. From the look on their faces behind the counter, it was a much larger tip than we thought it was. We left happy in the knowledge that those big smiles were genuine. We had given them a little happiness in what appeared to be a grim and challenging existence.

We left down the narrow staircase and poured out into the street as the cold hit us in the face. The weather forecast said it was minus twenty centigrade. Still, in all honesty, once it gets past zero, it just feels cold, very cold but indistinguishable how cold. The only factor is how long you can walk before it gets too cold to continue. In this instance, it wasn't long, and we were less than 50 yards around the corner before we found another bar.

This was a narrow street doorway leading into a long narrow bar inside. It was just enough to fit a row of small tables on one side and have space to walk past them to the bar at the far end. We were pleased to see a beer on one table. However, most occupants appeared to be drinking shorts and, inevitably, vodka. We were motioned to sit at a table by the barman, who immediately came over to take our order. We were pleased to find that his English was slightly more advanced than our previous barmaid's as he offered us vodka. Three beers, please we replied.

"Sorry, no beer, only spirits after 7 'o'clock" was his response. This time we ordered the vodkas first and discussed with him afterwards as we drank. Some locals on the adjacent table also joined in substituting English words here and there, sometimes right, sometimes wrong, but generally moving us in the right direction.

We never did find out if this was a local law, whether it was temporary because of local shortages, or if there was another more profound reason for this strange rule. Finally, we confirmed the most crucial fact: we could not get a beer anywhere after 7 pm.

The conclusion was that if we were drinking vodka, we could do it anywhere, so it would be better within walking distance of the ship for the end of the evening. So, it was a taxi back to a bar close to the shipyard, where we ended up being invited to a wedding by the wonderful local people.

At the end of the night, one thing was left to do before returning to the ship. We had each changed $10 for local currency at eight times the legal rate, and despite our drinking and taxis, we still had most of it left. This meant we had to give it away, giving us the perfect opportunity to put a collection in for the bride and groom and leave the rest as a tip for the bar staff. This was because, in the iron curtain port of Gdansk, we were searched on leaving the dock and money was recorded to compare with what we took back in. If we took more back, it was proof that we had exchanged on the black market and would be arrested.

We entered the port with drunken smiles, aware that we were all clear of money, and as the machine gun-carrying security staff questioned us, we realised they were smiling. They were aware of the ploys that bent the rules and looked genuinely happy that we had enjoyed a night in their country.

It was a realisation that all people, even those carrying machine guns for the state, want to be people, not numbers or Citizens, just people. Years later, as the Soviet Union collapsed, I thought of those people and cheered for them, yet now I despair at the attitude of present-day Britain. At some stage in recent history, Polish and other nationalities have become unwanted foreigners rather than the long-lost friends that they truly are.

A LETTER FROM VALLETTA
15/12/83 – 28/01/83

Even though the timing of the appointment letter that arrived in early December 1983 was appropriate, the fact that it arrived at all was a surprise to me.

Less than two months earlier, I had left M.V. Magdalena in Malta after a trip of five months, yet here was an instruction to re-join the same ship in Malta. My surprise was because the last month of my trip was spent laid up in Valletta Harbour pending the sale of the ship. Prior to that, in January 1983, I had left the M.V. Matina in Jeddah after delivering her to new owners, and I had expected Magdalena to have met the same fate.

Clearly, she had survived, but judging by the details within the joining instructions, it was only a temporary reprieve. I was to join a skeleton crew of nine officers on a ship that had been mothballed for three months.

Stepping off the plane into 17°c of Maltese winter sunshine ten days before Christmas was a little compensation for leaving home so close to the festive season. Joining a laid-up ship was also far less stressful than joining a seagoing one. I already knew the ship was moored in the majestic Valletta harbour. Although it was opposite the city itself, it had great postcard views of the city that tourists would pay a fortune for. Alas, the city was over twenty minutes away in a taxi and nearly 40 in a typical post-war Maltese bus. I also knew the real benefit of the quiet industrial area we were in was that the winery was two minutes away from the ship.

The winery was an exaggerated description of a large industrial unit with a service counter that sold local red or white wines by the case. The price best described the quality of the wine. Red wine was 40p a bottle and white wine 35p, and those prices included a 10p deposit on the empty bottle, which we always returned. With just twelve of us on board the ship, it was a regular trip every other day. Return two empty cases and pick up a case of red and a case of white. Total cost £6.60p. Sunshine and cheap wine, what more do you need for a good Christmas in Malta?

The answer to that question was a girlfriend. When I joined the ship, several officers had their wives living on board. This was a regular entitlement but rarely taken advantage of due to family commitments of children and the boredom of wives alone at sea whilst their husbands worked twelve hours a day. However, a ship moored in the beautiful city of Valletta over Christmas was a completely different proposition. The daytime was spent servicing the ship and services to keep it seaworthy and ready to sail, but every night and weekend was our own, an unknown luxury when sailing deep sea.

I bonded quickly with others on board due to the small numbers and the need to self-cater. With no catering crew on board, we had full access to the galley, and one of us had the daily duty of preparing a meal for the rest, which consisted of eight officers and three wives on board. The disasters were surprisingly outnumbered by the successful meals prepared, whilst the shared experience was an unexpected bonus.

The other unexpected bonus was the girlfriend option. The second mate had joined just before me and had used a loophole to get permission for his fiancé to stay over Christmas. I saw an opportunity and made the same request, and within one phone call to my girlfriend of six months, she had become my temporary fiancé with a flight booked to Malta. Both fiancés arrived several days later in time for New Year. Unfortunately, we had celebrated Christmas more enthusiastically than we should have and greeted them at the airport with broken ribs and a broken arm. My broken ribs were painful but hidden, whilst the second mate's left arm was visibly covered in a plaster cast. Our worry was not about our girlfriends finding out about the injuries but more about how we got them.

It all started with a poor-quality black and white photocopy of my driving licence. My licence had been sent off to have speeding points added, so I brought what I expected would be a useless photocopy with me. Strangely only the second mate and I had any licence at all when we decided to hire a car. With more hope than belief, I entered the hire office and was extremely surprised to walk out with the keys to a mini. Like all the hire cars on the island of Malta, it was a little old and battered, had one window wiper and was wrapped in black and yellow striped tape around the middle, similar to the police hazard tape at a crime scene. I believed this was to warn all the local drivers that it was a hire car, and unlike the local drivers, it was likely to stop at junctions and follow the rules of the road.

We soon learnt to drive like locals and visited many parts of the island with great success until we ventured to St Julian's Bay one evening for pizza. The pizza in question was so big that it filled the table, and there were still leftovers after being shared between the four of us. There was, however, no leftover beer despite the copious amounts we had drunk before and after our pizza blowout. This would not normally be a problem as we had agreed that the second mate, Paul, would be the nominated driver before the evening started. The problem was that Paul had forgotten to reduce his drinking, and none of us had noticed until we reached the car at the end of the evening. Unfortunately, all four of us were so drunk we hadn't noticed how drunk Paul was, and honestly, we didn't care. We just wanted to get back to the ship and had a car to do it in.

The mini was old but great fun to drive and felt very at home on an island where all the locals drove like Wacky Racers. It lacked a window wiper and any seatbelts, and the rear passengers would rattle around in the back over the bumpy roads and tight bends. Thirty miles an hour felt like sixty, and every trip was a thrilling but enjoyable white-knuckle ride. Twenty minutes into our ride home, in a drunken state, we were cheering every pothole and bend, encouraging Paul to keep the wild ride going. We were almost within sight of the ship, hurtling towards the last roundabout when someone challenged him to try a four-wheel drift. Of course, any sober driver knows that a front-wheel car cannot do a 4-wheel drift, but that didn't stop us from trying.

The next thing I remember was being slumped in the back seat and completely disoriented. All four of us were still in the car and, thankfully, conscious and talking. The car was stopped in the middle of the roundabout, having hit the small brick wall in the central island. Our first instinct was to drive on, but several attempts to start the car resulted in nothing at all. When we all managed to get out of the car, it became clear why it would not start. The front right wing had lost an argument with the brick wall and was completely wrecked. In addition to this, the engine had dropped off its mounting on that side and was resting on the road surface. The car was obviously terminal, so we retreated to the safety of the pavement to assess our own injuries. The combination of alcohol and adrenaline caused by shock appeared to have numbed us to any pain to such an extent that we felt fit enough to push the car to the pavement and clear the road.

Pushing a car with a bent wheel and engine on the floor is not easy for the most organised and sober group of people, and we were definitely neither. Luckily ten minutes later, our guardian angel turned up to offer assistance.

"Do you want some help?" we heard from behind us. We turned to see a tall, middle-aged man approaching, having parked his car nearby.

"Oh yes, please," we said in unison. "We had a little accident."

"I can see that. What happened?" he replied.

"Not familiar with the roads", responded Paul quickly.

"So where are you heading to? Do you need a lift?"

"Thanks for the offer, but we are walking distance from the ship now."

"Ah! English Seafarers, let me help you move this car to safety. Are you all ok?"

Having helped move the car to a safe location and confirmed that we were all in good health, our guardian angel introduced himself and left us his business card. He said I work just down the road. So if you have any problems tomorrow, just call me.

The card read 'Chief Inspector, Paulo Police Station.' Now that's what I call a police service.

The next day we visited the scene of the crime and could not believe the state of the car that we had tried to drive away in. I called the car hire company to explain that a tow truck was probably insufficient and that a crane and trailer may be more appropriate. Amazingly they also provided a replacement car for the duration of the hire period. I suspect the explanation of the Chief Inspector's involvement and showing his business card may have had some influence on their excellent service.

Having my girlfriend and a car was the icing on the cake for a wonderful fortnight in Malta. Just two weeks later, I also left for home on 28th January, not knowing where the future would take me or the company. I was expecting a long period of leave or even redundancy, but I suddenly found myself back on a ship within two weeks. On February 16th, I joined the same ship again but this time in Cadiz.

I was now working under the parent company of United Brands instead of Fyffes, but the biggest difference was the ship. Despite it being the same Magdalena that I knew and loved, the name on the hull now read M.V. Barrydale, and the red ensign on the stern had been replaced with a Panamanian flag.

I had sold my soul to the devil in order to gain sufficient sea time to study for my Chief Engineers Certificate. I needed three and a half months to qualify and accepted a trip as Second Engineer under a foreign flag to get it.

The trip lasted a very long six months. Whilst The predominantly Chinese Crew and Indian Officers were capable and lovely people, there was a massive gulf in the social life onboard. I had always been aware of how important that was in the harsh working environment at sea, but that trip really highlighted it, and I decided to leave the sea forever.

After the trip, the company called me to the London head office, offered to fund my study leave, and sent me to Japan. There I would stand by the construction of a new ship and do the maiden voyage alongside my favourite Chief Engineer. I listened with interest. I was tempted when they promised me the Chief's job after the maiden voyage. Then I remembered my last trip. So, I left and funded myself to achieve my Chief Engineers Certificate.

I realised that seagoing was about something other than money or seeing the world. It was about people. Meeting people. Socialising with those people. Making best friends for life or sometimes just for a few months. It was about baring all to a friend who will be there to save your skin one day, and then you may never meet again. It is about remembering them, remembering those great times together and experiences that money can't buy. It is about writing down the few memories I can still recall so that my children and grandchildren know that one day I was a young man too.

I had a life and experiences. I have been there and done it. The world is very different now, but life and adventures are still out there, and I encourage you all to go and find them. You will never regret it. I certainly don't.

Seagoing Schedule

Shaw Saville

S.S. Hardwick Grange (Cadet)
Join Sheerness UK	25/10/76 – 29/10/76
London East India Dock	29/10/76 – 17/11/76
Panama Canal transit	
Wellington, New Zealand	18/12/76 – 08/01/77
Picton New Zealand	09/01/77 – 12/01/77
Dunedin New Zealand	13/01/77 – 20/01/77
Bluff New Zealand	20/01/77 – 17/02/77
Panama Canal transit	
Pay off Avonmouth UK	22/03/77

M.V. Laurentic (Cadet)
Depart London	30/05/77
Panama Canal transit	
Pitcairn Island (mail run)	
Lyttleton New Zealand	01/06/77 – 18/06/77
Picton New Zealand	18/06/77 – 22/06/77
New Plymouth, New Zealand	23/06/77 – 02/07/77
Bluff New Zealand	05/07/77 – 09/07/77
Balboa Panama	27/07/77
Panama Canal transit	
Cristobal Panama	29/07/77
Newhaven UK	10/08/77

Shaw Saville

M.V. Laurentic (Cadet/Junior Engineer)

Depart Sheerness	06/07/78
Gulfport Mississippi USA	18/07/78 – 21/07/78
Tampa, Florida USA	22/07/78 – 23/07/78
Le Havre France	03/08/78 – 04/08/78
Rotterdam Holland	05/08/78 – 06/08/78
Sheerness UK	07/08/78 – 09/08/78
Valleyfield USA/Quebec	19/08/78 – 20/08/78
St Lawrence seaway transit	
Kenosha Wisconsin USA	24/08/78 – 01/09/78
St Lawrence seaway transit	
Le Havre France	13/09/78 – 16/09/78
Rotterdam Holland	17/09/78 – 19/09/78
Sheerness UK	20/09/78 – 26/09/78
Valleyfield USA/Quebec	07/10/78 - 07/10/78
St Lawrence seaway transit	
Kenosha USA (Chicago)	10/10/78 – 18/10/78
St Lawrence seaway transit	
Le Havre France	03/11/78 – 04/11/78
Antwerp Belgium	05/11/78 – 06/11/78
Rotterdam Holland	07/11/78 – 08/11/78
Sheerness UK	08/11/78

Shaw Saville

M.V. Zealandic (Junior Engineer)

Sheerness UK	18/12/78 – 21/12/78
Gulfport Mississippi USA	04/01/79 – 09/01/79
Tampa, Florida USA	11/01/79 – 13/01/79
Le Havre France	25/01/79 – 29/01/79
Rotterdam Holland	30/01/79 – 31/01/79
Sheerness UK	01/02/79 – 03/02/79
Gulfport Mississippi USA	19/02/79 – 25/02/79
Tampa, Florida USA	26/02/79 – 03/03/79
Le Havre France	16/03/79 – 20/03/79
Hamburg Germany	20/03/79
Rotterdam Holland	21/03/79 – 24/03/79
Sheerness UK	25/03/79 – 30/03/79
Gulfport USA (New Orleans)	11/04/79 – 17/04/79
Tampa USA	19/04/79 – 20/04/79
Le Havre France	03/05/79 – 08/05/79
Rotterdam Holland	09/05/79 – 11/05/79
Sheerness UK	12/05/79 – 14/05/79

Fyffes Line

M.V. Magdalena (Junior Engineer)

Avonmouth UK	11/11/79 – 14/11/79
Turbo Columbia	24/11/79 – 28/11/79
Cristobal Panama	28/11/79
Southampton UK	09/12/79 – 10/12/79
Bremerhaven Germany	12/12/79 – 13/12/79
Keil canal transit	
Gdansk Poland	15/12/79 – 20/12/79
Keil canal transit	
Bremen Germany	22/12/79 – 29/12/79
Almirante Panama	10/01/80 – 11/01/80
Cristobal Panama	12/01/80
Panama Canal transit	
Armuelles Panama	13/01/80 – 16/01/80
Golfito Costa Rica	17/01/80 – 24/01/80
Balboa Panama	25/01/80
Panama Canal transit	
Cristobal Panama	26/01/80
Oslo Norway	08/02/20 – 11/02/20
Gothenburg Sweden	12/02/80 – 13/02/80
Rotterdam Holland Pay off	15/02/80

Fyffes Line

M.V. Darien (Junior Engineer/4th Engineer)

Hobart Tasmania	09/05/80
Port Huon Tasmania	10/05/80 – 12/05/80
Beauty Point Tasmania	13/05/80 – 20/05/80
Perth (bunkers)	
Suez Egypt	18/06/80
Suez Canal transit	
Port Said Egypt	09/06/80
Gibraltar C/E pay off	13/06/80
Hamburg Germany	17/06/80 – 18/06/80
Rotterdam Holland	18/06/80 – 21/06/80
Sheerness UK	21/06/80 – 26/06/80
Promoted to 4th Eng.	22/06/80
Turbo Columbia	07/07/80 – 08/07/80
Puerto Limon Cost Rica	10/07/80 – 11/07/80
Galveston, Texas USA	15/07/80 – 16/07/80
Gulfport Mississippi USA	17/07/80 – 21/06/80
Almirante Panama	27/07/80 – 30/07/80
Oslo Norway	11/08/80 – 12/08/80
Gothenburg Sweden	13/08/80
Sheerness UK	15/08/80 – 17/08/80
Barry Island drydock UK	18/08/80 – 05/09/80
Hamburg Germany	08/09/80 – 24/09/80
St John New Brunswick Canada	01/10/80 – 02/10/80
Halifax, Nova Scotia Canada	03/10/80 – 04/10/80
Tela Honduras	09/10/80 – 10/10/80
Cristobal Panama	12/10/80 – 15/10/80
Panama Canal transit	
Golfito Costa Rica	17/10/80 – 23/10/80
Valparaiso Chile Pay off	29/10/80

Fyffes Line

M.V. Matina (4th Engineer)

Galveston, Texas USA	28/12/80 – 30/12/80
Armuelles Panama	05/01/81 – 07/01/81
Bremerhaven Germany (dock strike)	21/08/81 – 10/02/82
Hamburg Germany	11/02/81 – 12/02/81
Tela Honduras	26/02/81 – 28/02/81
Almirante Panama	02/03/81 – 03/03/81
Turbo Columbia	04/03/81 – 08/03/81
Cristobal Panama	09/03/81
Panama Canal transit	
Golfito Costa Rica	11/03/81 – 12/03/81
Armuelles Panama	13/03/81 – 17/03/81
Balboa Panama	19/03/81
Panama Canal transit	
Livorno Italy	02/04/81 – 08/04/81
Armuelles Panama	23/03/81 – 24/03/81
Santa Marta Columbia	29/04/81 – 30/04/81
Genoa Italy	13/05/81 – 16/05/81
Cristobal Panama	28/05/81
Turbo Columbia	30/05/81
Sheerness UK	Unknown
Oslo Norway	Unknown
Gothenburg Sweden	Unknown
Avonmouth pay off	01/07/81

Fyffes Line

M.V. Magdalena (3rd Engineer)

Antwerp Belgium	15/01/82
Oslo Norway	16/01/82 – 17/01/82
Gothenburg Sweden	19/01/81 – 20/01/82
St John, New Brunswick Canada	29/01/82 – 01/02/82
Tela Honduras	06/02/82 – 13/02/82
Port Everglades (Fort Lauderdale)	15/02/82
Oslo Norway	28/02/82 – 01/03/82
Gothenburg Sweden	02/03/82 – 03/03/82
Bremerhaven Germany	04/03/82 – 06/03/82
Armuelles Panama	19/03/82 – 20/03/82
Golfito Costa Rica	21/03/82
Salerno Italy	05/04/82 – 08/04/82
Beirut Lebanon	11/04/82 – 16/04/82
Alexandria Egypt (Pyramids)	17/04/84 – 19/04/82
Cristobal Panama	2/05/82
Almirante Panama	06/05/82 - 07/05/82
Antwerp Belgium	26/05/82

Fyffes Line

M.V. Matina (3rd Engineer)

Albany, New York USA	30/08/82
Armuelles Panama	09/08/82 – 10/08/82
Salerno Italy (Pompei)	27/09/82
Naples Italy	29/08/82
Salerno Italy	30/09/82 – 07/10/82
Suez Canal transit	10/10/82
Jeddah Saudi Arabia	12/10/82 – 16/10/82
Suez Canal transit	17/10/82 – 18/10/82
Valletta Malta	20/10/82 – 25/10/82
Savannah, Georgia USA	08/11/82 – 10/11/82
Tela Honduras	15/11/82 – 28/11/82
Port Everglades Florida USA	31/11/82
Gothenburg Sweden	13/12/82 – 14/12/82
Oslo Norway	15/12/82
Antwerp Belgium (Dry dock – ship sold)	19/12/82 – 05/01/83
Agadir Morocco	08/01/83 – 10/01/83
Jeddah Saudi Arabia	30/01/83

Fyffes Line

M.V. Magdalena (3ʳᵈ Engineer)

Antwerp Belgium	20/05/83
Tela Honduras	31/05/83
Almirante Panama	02/06/83 – 03/06/83
Cristobal Panama	04/06/83
Tela Honduras	06/06/83
Gothenburg Sweden	19/06/83 – 20/06/83
Oslo Norway	21/06/83
Antwerp Belgium	24/06/83
Hamburg Germany	26/06/83 – 29/06/83
Port Everglades Florida USA	10/07/83
Tela Honduras	13/07/83 – 17/07/83
Limon Costa Rica	20/07/83
Gulfport Mississippi	25/07/83 – 27/07/83
Limon Costa Rica	01/08/83
Turbo Columbia	04/08/83
Livorno Italy (Pisa)	5 days
Valletta Malta (lay-up)	1 month until 20/09/83

M.V. Magdalena

Malta Lay up   15/12/83 – 28/01/83

United Brands Foreign Flag

M.V. Barrydale (2nd Engineer)

Feb – August 84
Cadiz Spain	16/02/84
Lisbon	Unknown
Italy	Unknown
Albany	Unknown
Tela	Unknown
Beirut	Unknown
Salerno Italy	31/08/84

Printed in Great Britain
by Amazon